Steps to Tranquility

How to Stay Sane in the Digital Age

VASUDEVAN RAJARAM

9 Steps to Tranquility: How to Stay Sane in the Digital Age

Copyright ©2024 by Vasudevan Rajaram

Published by Bodhi Publishing.

Paperback ISBN: 979-8-9917718-0-1
eISBN: 979-8-9917718-1-8

Cover and Interior Design: GKS Creative
Editing: Judith West
Proofreading: Kim Bookless
Project Management: The Cadence Group

To my wife, Usha, and daughter, Pooja

CONTENTS

FOREWORD

I HAVE GREAT SATISFACTION in writing the foreword to this book—
9 Steps to Tranquility by Dr. Vasudevan Rajaram. The satisfaction arises
from various factors. One, tranquility is a valuable quality to have,
acquire, and develop, at any time, for any human being. Particularly so
in these times of rapid technological and social changes, turbulence,
and stress. Two, the book has evolved out of the personal experiences
of the author, Dr. Rajaram. He had gone through the usual current
style of stressful working and living, and consequent health issues.
Then he turned to meditation, work-life balance, etc. Three, he was
confident enough in these lessons to venture teaching them to his own
daughter when she was young. She has benefited. She is a successful
professional now. Four, he has drawn upon three great world religions,
and not just his own, Hinduism. Five, he has also relied upon recent,
modern academic research, with appropriate methodology, into
mindful meditation and related topics. Six, he has chosen as examples
of tranquility the lives of highly effective leaders, such as Mahatma
Gandhi, Nelson Mandela, and others. Seven, he is himself following
these 9 Steps—practicing what he is preaching—which should inspire
credibility and confidence in the readers.

The author has listed values in essay 1. Some are relatively easier
to practice than others. Some are harder. Perhaps the most important,
and also the most difficult, is Self-Discipline. We become creatures
of habit. The human condition is that bad habits are easier to pick up

and difficult to drop. Good habits are the opposite of this: harder to imbibe and easy to shed. Bad habits give us some immediate pleasure and require not much effort. We need to strengthen our will power, to make the right choices. An important way is regular practice of good habits—especially meditation.

The second most difficult value may be applying these values in the Digital Age. Even in pre-digital times, application lagged behind comprehension. Much more so in this digital age. The cell phone, tablet, laptop, and similar devices are too much with us. One needs great self-control to attend to the important and ignore the trivial, or lower priority, items. The third difficulty is to retain our value for these and similar values. We may rationalize our failure to practice by devaluing the values themselves!

In essay 2, the heart of the book, the author shows how to implement the 9 Steps. You are fortunate if, early in your life, your parents and teachers give you the right guidance. If not, how long can we blame parents and teachers for our problems? When do we take charge of our own life? At 18, in many countries, one can vote, marry, and join the armed forces. So, at 18, or soon after that, one must take responsibility for one's own personality and life. This essay draws from different religions, preachers, gurus, and others. It also cites academic research and writing. You may have read some of them. You may plan to catch up with more.

It is useful to develop two things to guide you in life. One, your Professional Mission, in whichever profession you are. Two, your Life Vision: What do you want to be appreciated and remembered for? Your contribution to the community, alma mater, society, etc., is as important as, if not more than, your professional and financial career success. Accepting, managing, and learning from some inevitable failures, setbacks, and disappointments in life is important. This requires the ability to stand outside and examine yourself, as a witness would do. Assess yourself on your level of ambition or indolence. Ambition is better. But it should be moderated by selflessness and sharing. We come into the world and flourish in it, not entirely by our own efforts. We owe debts to many. We must discharge them, as much as possible.

Readers of this book may come to it with one of three attitudes. Some already know of many things in the book. For them, the book is a confirmation. They may intensify their practice. The second group may have an open mind. Most of them are likely to be convinced by the book and may start to practice many of its valuable suggestions. The third group may be skeptical. While the entire book may help them overcome their skepticism, essay 3 may be of particular interest and impact for them. In this essay, "The Scientific Basis for Tranquility," the author cites extensive evidence from scientific, academic research into meditation and its impact on our physiology (especially the mind) and on levels of anxiety and depression, inflammation, blood pressure, migraine and other pains, lung capacity, concentration, sleep quality, and sense of well-being. The research findings cited in this chapter will also be useful to the first two types of readers, as reinforcement.

Having cited scientific evidence in support of tranquility in essay 3, the author goes on in essay 4 to deal with its spiritual basis. There, he draws upon three major world religions: Hinduism, Islam, and Christianity. He shows how each of these religions, in its own way, can lead us to tranquility. The reader may stay rooted and benefit from her/his own religion and, at the same time, get reinforcement from similar thoughts in the other religions. Even agnostics and atheists need tranquility. They can benefit from the spiritual, moral, and behavioral guidance of all, some, or any one of these religions, leaving aside the religious and ritualistic aspects. A key idea is to enjoy material comforts and pleasures up to a point and transcend them to also relish and benefit from spiritual awareness and actions. Earn, enjoy, save, invest, etc., but also donate, regularly, some part of your accumulating wealth. Experience not only the pleasure of consumption, but also the joy of giving. It is creditable that the author himself, being a Hindu, has done full, respectful justice to all the other major religions, capturing the main tenets each.

Essay 5 deals with the importance of tranquility and how to capture it. In stressful situations, it can help us to think calmly, analyze, and prioritize our actions. It can help us cope with the inevitable ups and downs of life. There is a facile assumption that only the downward swings are a problem. The upward swings can also be a hazard. Tranquility can help us to both not go under and not go overboard. Similar is the unavoidable duality of happiness and sorrow. Enjoy the happiness while it lasts. Develop the aptitudes and skills to find happiness. Don't repress sorrow. Experience it and then come back to tranquility. Likewise, in health, we need both physical fitness and emotional stability. Lack of tranquility affects the mind, and a disturbed mind reduces physical health. Many illnesses have a psychosomatic element. Then, there is stress. It is unavoidable. No stress or very low stress may mean that the individual is underutilizing her potential. Reasonable aspirations and stretch goals will produce some stress. Tranquility will help to cope with such optimal, productive stress. The author shares his own priority ordering in his successful career — health first, family next. And, of course, work, enhanced by good health and a happy family. Financial success has its place but not at the cost of life's valuable intangibles.

The author looks at the lives and lessons of six tranquil world leaders. At the top of the list is Mahatma Gandhi, about whom Einstein said that future generations will wonder if such a human existed! He took upon himself the stress of fighting apartheid in South Africa, with nonviolence. He got Indian independence through peaceful means. It was the start of decolonization of many other countries around the world. He held no political office. His power was moral. He continues to be a beacon for activists for peace, environment, social justice, etc.

Nelson Mandela was greatly inspired by Gandhi. He had no bitterness against South African whites. He pursued truth and reconciliation. He could build a "Rainbow Nation." Just as Gandhi said, "We love the British. But, we don't want British rule." Mandela urged his people not to take revenge against former oppressors. Barack Obama exemplified quiet confidence, hope, audacity, and an excellent temperament, at all stages of his rapid rise. When he became the first Black president of the United States, people were happy not only in the U.S., but in the whole democratic world. I recall the public excitement in India at every milestone of his success—nomination; election as president, twice; his reforms and policies. It was as if one of us had won. The author gives a long list of values and qualities that helped Obama.

After the above examples of three political leaders, the author takes up the life of love and service to the poorest of the poor, Mother Teresa of the Missionaries of Charity, Calcutta (now Kolkata). Having lived in that fascinating city for some years, in the 1960s and later in the 1970s, I am familiar with her good work. For her lifelong dedicated service, she was canonized.

To some, Warren Buffet may appear an improbable choice. I think it is an inspired selection. Like power, money can also corrupt, beyond a point. Buffett made lots of money for himself and his shareholders. But it did not make him arrogant. Nor did it corrupt him. He has kept giving a lot of it away. He earned the title of "The Sage of Omaha."

The last, but not the least, of the six role models is the late Dr. Abdul Kalam. He is very well known in India and among the Indian diaspora worldwide. He was a professional scientist. He made a great contribution in defense research. He conducted successful nuclear tests. He was himself a man of peace. He understood India's need for a nuclear deterrent capability. He was more interested in nuclear power for development. He was a very popular and loved president of India, a nonparty political post. He focused on youth and on "igniting" their minds.

In his Conclusions, the author briefly recapitulates his own personal benefit from the 9 Steps, and the resultant tranquility. He urges readers to integrate these steps into their lives. The keywords are: *Start Now*.

I commend this practical book to youth around the world. I hope it will be translated into several languages. I urge parents and relatives to give this book as a gift to young people. I hope teachers, especially of the social sciences, will recommend this book to their college and school libraries. Self-management is the foundation of a better society, with peace and welfare for all.

New Delhi
Dr. Mrityunjay Athreya, PhD (Harvard)
October 2023
Institutional Mentor

INTRODUCTION

No one saves us but ourselves. No one can and no one may.
We ourselves must walk the path.
— THE BUDDHA

TRANQUILITY IS DEFINED by Merriam-Webster as "freedom from agitation of the mind and spirit." It also defines it as freedom from disturbance or turmoil. Synonyms suggested include calm, serenity, placidity, and peace. Wikipedia calls *tranquility* a calm state of mind. For me, tranquility is an inner peace that allows me to think clearly and find solutions to problems that I face in life. It has allowed me to navigate any life situation without losing my temper and to be kind to all with whom I interact. It has allowed me to stay sane in the digital information age and achieve both professional and personal success. It has made me more spiritual and helped me work toward Moksha, or Nirvana, the total freedom that allows you to accept the world as it is and avoid passing judgment on others.

This book arises from my desire to share my insights with others and help them become calmer under the difficult situations we face at work, in personal relationships, and at home.

The digital age has defined our lives in a relatively short time. I remember the first several years of my career, in the 1970s and '80s, when the only means of electronic business communication was by phone or fax. Emails were not widely used until the system was introduced in the mid-1990s. So once I left work at 5:00 p.m., there were no phone calls to handle until I went to work the next morning at 8:00 a.m. In the 1990s, emails became common in business, but no one expected responses during nonworking hours. In the early 2000s, however, smartphones were introduced, and with the advent of the Apple iPhone in 2007, the digital revolution was off at a maddening pace. The 24/7 communication cycle had begun.

My daughter is a lawyer and is tied up even on weekends, as her clients communicate day and night and expect responses immediately. At home, my son-in-law constantly monitors his phone for messages from his colleagues in the space industry and does not get enough sleep. In the office, he works with two computer screens at once. My daughter constantly checks her cell phone while we are enjoying a game of cards. So even family time has become hostage to the digital revolution.

In more recent years, audio and video streaming services have proliferated, tempting even the most disciplined person to overindulge in the entertainment they offer. These services, combined with the continuous workplace use of digital communications, have shaped the lives of today's young people.

In the earlier years of my own career, I, too, believed that getting ahead meant I had to be focused on work even while I was at home and during weekends. I worked hard for a small business where, I was told, I could become a partner in three years. So even on a family vacation, I could be found doing things that contributed to the success of the business. Finally, after three years of all that hard work, came the announcement that the company owner didn't want to make me a partner after all and I should look for another job.

To say that I was stunned would be an understatement. But this *did* turn out to be the catalyst for me to start my own company in 1986. And I worked just as hard to make my company successful. Then, in 1989, as I was diligently running my business in addition to attending law school in the evenings, all while trying to do the best for my family, I fell ill and needed surgery.

That development was a major eye-opener for me—so much so that afterward, I decided that taking care of my health and spending time with family were going to be more important than work. By coming to understand the importance of work-life balance and learning to adjust my attitude toward work, I discovered the things that I will be describing in this book.

My motivation for writing this book came from my daughter. She and I spent a lot of time together in her early years (before she became a teenager and, of course, didn't need my help anymore). When she was very young, though, I taught her the values that would be important in her life, as well as how she could handle the many tasks in a busy world without becoming stressed out. Later, when she started her law practice in Los Angeles, she told me that the values and lessons I taught her at an early age were useful in her demanding law practice. She also said that although she saw a lot of self-help books in stores, none of them presented an approach to tranquility as clearly and simply as the steps I had taught her. She urged me to write about my pathway, and that became the 9 Steps of this book, which I dedicate to her.

At my daughter's urging and from my own beliefs and experience, therefore, I've written this book to remind you, my readers, how much more life offers than what the digital revolution has brought about. Instead of our being constantly bombarded with information at work and at home, we can decide to have a tranquil life with a balance between life and work. We can pay attention to our health, eat right, and get enough sleep. And while it is up to each person to draw limits for himself or herself, the guidelines in this book show how nine simple steps in life can help tune out the world's digital din and remain tranquil within.

These pages will also examine the idea that money does not buy happiness and demonstrate how good health and healthy relationships contribute to happiness. The message here also stresses that while material things may bring a temporary sense of joy, true joy comes in living a meaningful life, making a difference to humanity, and giving your time, talent, and treasure to others in need. Indeed, true joy includes spending some time every week in spiritual pursuits.

In essay 1, we'll look in some detail at the values I believe one should base one's life on. Although many of us profess to have values, we often do not place much value on them—especially when confronted with difficult situations at work or home. The nine values I'll discuss are age-old and do not change with time or with the circumstances we may face. Many of them are interconnected, and if you hold a few key values, the others will likely follow naturally.

Essential values include, for one, not harming others and, for another, speaking the truth under all circumstances. After all, consider that we ourselves would never wish to be harmed. And consider further that if the truth were only told sometimes—say, only under oath or only when it was convenient—then it wouldn't be worth anything. And both of these values, if they became widespread in society, would surely lead to a tranquil culture. The number of police could be reduced, with law and order still preserved, since most people would behave based on two central values.

Essay 2 is the crux of the book, as it details the 9 Steps to follow toward tranquility in our lives:

- Cultivate Discipline.
- Be True to Yourself.
- Put Health First.
- Refine Your Attitude Toward Work.
- Practice Daily Meditation/Quiet Time.
- Build Work-Life Balance.
- Serve Others.
- Live a Purposeful Life.
- Always See the Big Picture.

I introduce examples from my personal life to help explain each of the 9 Steps, in hopes that my experience may guide others in their own practice of these steps to attain tranquility.

Because I have always benefited from daily meditation, I was inclined to research the scientific basis for meditation and how it can help us to remain tranquil in our busy day-to-day lives. Essay 3 approaches this topic and the work done at the University of Wisconsin by Dr. Richard Davidson and his colleagues, and others. It also refers to sources from the Eastern tradition of meditation and shows how the physical and psychological benefits of meditation justify the daily time that we need to set aside for it. And though morning and just before sleep are particularly good times to meditate, the key is to practice it regularly to calm the mind and make it productive.

Essay 4 highlights the spiritual foundations of tranquility found in the traditions of Hinduism, Islam, and Christianity. All religions emphasize that true happiness arises from treating others well and doing the right thing in all transactions that we face in our day-to-day activities. The importance of ethical values and belief in God are stressed in this essay. When I was researching this essay, I was pleasantly surprised by the similarity reflected in the major religions as to the ways to remain tranquil and live a productive life. No one religion outshone another since all lead to the same goal: true inner happiness under all circumstances. For those whose happiness lies in the acquisition of creature comforts, or who measure success by the amount of money they have instead of the impact of their lives on others in society, this essay can be especially useful. It also reminds all that whatever religion we follow, we have to diligently practice its teachings to remain tranquil.

The benefits of remaining tranquil are discussed in essay 5. You might suppose such benefits to be self-evident, but they are sometimes more subtle than you would expect. They include, for example, good physical and mental health, quality relationships with family and friends, and success in your professional life. We chase happiness at all costs in the outside world, but my work in this book is to show that true happiness lies in yourself, starting with personal discipline and your attitude toward work and your relationships. By emphasizing health and relationships, you pay less attention to material things, which give only temporary happiness. Looking carefully, you'll see that the benefits gained from becoming disciplined and remaining tranquil far outweigh the effort needed to gain them.

Essay 6 presents biographies of leaders who have made a huge impact on society while leading a nonetheless tranquil life through the many stresses they have faced in their work:

- Mohandas Karamchand Gandhi
- Nelson Mandela
- Barack Obama
- Mother Teresa
- Warren Buffett
- A. P. J. Kalam

These exemplary leaders have been especially meaningful in my life, and in this essay, I examine how their realization of tranquility served them and the people they led as they changed the world for the better.

In Conclusions, we wrap up all the ideas and actions covered in this book by reviewing the high points, illustrated by a few more stories and anecdotes. In closing, I once again urge you to practice the 9 Steps and discover how to benefit from the tranquility that will permeate your life.

Values-Based Living

No one can find inner peace except by working, not in a self-centered way, but for the whole human family.

— PEACE PILGRIM

U.S. peace activist and spiritual teacher

VALUES, IN A GENERAL SENSE, refer to any system of beliefs or standards, whether they're considered good or bad, righteous or corrupt. And some kind of values lie at the core of every life. In this book, in this essay, and indeed, in most of modern society's use of the term, values are a specific and highly desirable system of virtues, principles, and outlooks. Moving forward, our use of *values*—as in values-based living—is in the latter, specific meaning: values that provide guidance for a life that is ethical and purpose-driven. If we all lived a values-based life, surely community participation would increase and neighborhoods would grow strong. Values make up the foundation on which the steps to tranquility and true long-term happiness are built. In the following pages, we'll look closely at nine particular values that, when embraced, can help us find a tranquil life.

The values enumerated here are all interconnected, and diligently following one often leads quite naturally to another:

1. Develop consideration and respect for others.
2. Be honest.
3. Exercise compassion and charity.
4. Learn self-discipline.
5. Practice forbearance and anger management.
6. Look for goodness in others.
7. Don't gossip.
8. Abstain from jealousy.
9. Cultivate resilience.

It sounds like there's a lot to do to attain tranquility and peace of mind. And in fact, there is. And it is worth every bit of the effort you need to put in to develop and maintain these values, both as ends in themselves and as stepping stones along the path to tranquility.

We generally learn our values early in life, mostly at home from parents, grandparents, and other caregivers. I remember my parents and grandparents taught me the Golden Rule when I was only four years old: to treat everyone as I would like to be treated. And my grandmother taught me the value of charity, impressing upon me at a very young age that it is better to give than receive. Schoolteachers also frequently have a great influence. My elementary teachers steeped in us the value of honesty in studies and never to cheat on exams.

My elder brother taught me the value of doing my best and of leaving the result in God's hands. As I started my professional career, I gathered more about values as I dealt with fellow professionals, and the values of self-discipline and hard work became second nature to me. What became clear to me, and should be emerging to you, is that learning and living these values is an ongoing process. And the more closely we follow a values-based life, the more contented and tranquil we become.

1. Develop Consideration and Respect for Others

Each soul is potentially divine, as the great Hindu teacher Swami Vivekanada has taught, and we should treat everyone with respect and consideration of them as individuals, as well as in light of the circumstances in their life. If you follow the Golden Rule, respecting others and being considerate of them becomes easy and follows naturally. And when you interact with others, a smile and a kind word often leads the other person to respond similarly.

In life, both professionally and otherwise, I have found that being respectful and interested in others has helped me. What's more, by sharing your time and talent through volunteer activity in your community, you can enjoy a broader range of people and learn more about them. Caring for others less fortunate than you is a major pillar of a successful community and society, extending all the way to the national level.

In the 1982 book *Peace Pilgrim*,[1] Peace tells of deciding it was her calling to walk across the United States and spread her message of peace. It tells of how respecting and seeing the goodness in the people she met along the way provided her opportunities to share her message to thousands of fellow citizens. She was taken care of by strangers she met along her way, and she depended on their kindness for her food and shelter.

____

1 *Peace Pilgrim, Peace Pilgrim: Her Life and Work in Her Own Words* (Ocean Tree Books, 1982).

In her travels over 28 years in all parts of the United States, she encountered kindness and helped countless people improve their lives and find peace within themselves. She is a perfect example of how people from all walks of life react when you treat them with respect and love.

Peace Pilgrim relates the story of a drunk she met in a bar. He smiled at her. She smiled back. He said, "I should think you wouldn't even speak to me, but you smiled at me." She smiled again. She told him, "I'm not here to judge my fellow human beings. I'm here to love and serve." Suddenly, he was kneeling at her feet and saying, "Everyone else judged me, so I defended myself. You didn't judge me, so now I judge myself. I'm a no-good, worthless sinner! I've been squandering my money on liquor. I've been mistreating my family. I've been going from bad to worse!" Peace put her hand on his shoulder and said, "You are God's child, and you could act that way." He then threw the drink away and told Peace, "I swear to you I'll never touch that stuff again," and walked away. Peace reports that he has kept his word, has a good job, and is getting along well with his family.

Certainly an inspiring example of the power of kind words and respect for a fellow human being. And we, too, can avoid being judgmental in our relationships and help others improve at their own pace. No one is perfect, and it is better to be kind to others than be critical of them—better for them and better for us, in learning consideration and respect.

2. Be Honest

There is an old adage in India: "If you tell one lie, you have to tell a thousand lies to cover it up." Fortunately, you don't have to keep working so hard if you tell the truth the first time. All religions place great consequence on honest living, and it receives the most importance in the hierarchy of values. It is said to purify one's soul and lead to a tranquil life.

Honesty can mean saying what you mean and meaning what you say. It builds trust in your relationships and makes communication easy with your friends, spouse, and children. Honesty in families is important for building a strong relationship between spouses and between the spouses and their children. Untruth between spouses is the largest reason for divorce.

Many business relationships fail, too, because trust is broken by one party to the relationship. If you lie, you will almost certainly contradict yourself later. And to avoid the lie being detected, you'll have to invent many more lies, and soon you'll be lost within your lies. Politicians retain the trust of the electorate only by being straightforward with them. A lawful and just society is built on everyone being up front with each other.

Honesty helps you to avoid greed. I'm not talking about ambition, which, in moderation, can be a good and useful quality to fuel your progress in life. But greed is malignant and insatiable, and it ruins many lives. Greed finds you needing more and more, never being satisfied with what you have. It starts with a desire for something or someone that you want for your own. And if that desire is frustrated, it leads to anger. If fulfilled, the desire rises up again. As you satisfy one desire, others are lurking, demanding to be fulfilled—an easy thing to do in our consumer-oriented society.

Our needs are few, and our wants can be limitless. Honesty *with ourselves* can help us see that. We need to be able to recognize when our shopping list is based on what we think we need or on the latest gadgets in the electronics show. We can live in a three-bedroom house and be happy, instead of acquiring a six-bedroom house and being constantly stressed about the size of the mortgage. Similarly, buying a gas-guzzling expensive car when a more modest, less expensive car will better serve your needs is a kind of greedy self-deceit. So being aware of your budget and spending only on your actual needs, and saving enough for a rainy day, will help you practice the value of honesty.

When I was in elementary school, my teacher detected that I was not straightforward in answering her question, and she taught me a lesson on the importance of this trait. She asked me, "Did you copy from the student next to you?" I said, "No." Then she asked me if I glanced at his answer paper. I said, "Yes." She rebuked me gently, saying that the intent to copy by glancing at the next student's answer paper was as bad as copying. "Please don't do it again." This lesson in my fifth grade has stayed with me throughout my life. It has helped me in my career and in all my relationships, including building business relationships in India and the United States. It has allowed me to sleep well and stay healthy throughout my life. It has contributed to making my life stress-free and enjoying every relationship I have had over the years. So I urge you to develop this trait and avoid the path of lies that can surely lead down a slippery slope of broken relationships.

Honesty is the basis of trust among individuals, and trust increases cooperation and community building. Truth is especially important in the government to build trust among citizens and make sure citizens participate actively in a democracy. The secretiveness of dictatorial regimes impedes progress, and outright lies make the citizenry very jittery. The importance of truth was recognized by the Indian government when it was formed in 1947, with the national motto "Satyameva Jayate," meaning "Only Truth Wins." Whenever an Indian government did not speak truth to the public, it was defeated in the next election. Truth to power is an important aspect of a Free Press, which holds the government accountable. The press in the United States exposed the lie of Donald Trump about the COVID-19 pandemic, and he lost the reelection.

Some corporations have learned from experience that it is better to speak the truth about problems with their products, because covering up problems can lead to a company's eventual failure. We see more car companies issuing massive vehicle recalls for faults that could jeopardize safety or break the trust of customers. These companies would rather spend the money to fix the problem than lose their reputation and their market share. In 1982, when Johnson & Johnson faced the problem of tainted Tylenol tablets, they faced it truthfully, resolved the issue quickly, and did not suffer much financial loss. Building trust with employees, shareholders, and customers is key to every company, and speaking the truth about what is happening is better than trying to cover things up with lies.

3. Exercise Compassion and Charity

The word *compassion* comes originally from words meaning "to suffer together." Compassion is the feeling that arises when you see a person who is suffering and you feel motivated to do something to relieve the suffering. Compassion is a call to action using whatever resources you can muster. In times of natural calamity or human-made disaster, a community working together can help relieve the suffering of those affected. Many civic, national, and international organizations respond with compassion wherever people are suffering. As a member of the Lions Club, I know that this group sends out disaster relief funds to stricken communities and local members volunteer to do what they can to relieve people's distress.

Compassion results in acts of charity, the act of giving your time, talent, and treasure (that is, money) to those who are suffering. Personal experience has taught me that charity benefits the giver as much as, and sometimes more than, the recipient. Many people think of charity only as giving money, declaring that they don't have the resources to spare anything for the disadvantaged. But charity also includes giving your time and talent to those in your community less fortunate than you. When I was in my forties, I started spending two hours of my week to tutor and mentor inner-city children. And it made me very happy to see that these two hours every week helped a young girl who was planning to drop out of high school successfully enter a highly ranked local university. My passion for mentoring young people has stayed with me throughout my life.

Greater Good magazine is among a number of sources citing research on the biological basis of compassion: research that suggests compassion has a deep evolutionary purpose. When we feel compassion, our heart rate slows down, we secrete the "bonding hormone" oxytocin, and regions of the brain linked to empathy, caregiving, and feelings of pleasure light up, which results in us wanting to approach and care for other people. Perhaps you have experienced this as I have when encountering people who are not as fortunate as yourself. I try my best to help them however I can, mobilizing my connections and resources to try to improve their condition, whatever it is. This compassion-based action, this charity, not only benefits the recipient but contributes to my remaining tranquil and happy.

The twin values of compassion and charity may come to us through various channels. In Hinduism, for example, one of the holiest books, the Bhagavad Gita, teaches that charity, sacrifice, and penance purify the mind and lead to a tranquil life. I was taught when I was very young that helping others is the best way to live a useful life. Many people offer charity by volunteering their time for community service. For some, with careful planning, giving a small percentage of their income to the poor is possible. My father told me when I was in college that giving 2 percent of my income is a duty, and if I could do more, I should do so. Over the decades, my financial resources allowed me to give more, reaching 10 percent of my income in my fifth decade. But making what was a sacrifice of sorts clearly helped lead to tranquility on my part; over time, it went nearly unnoticed by me and did what I hope is considerable good for others.

4. Learn Self-Discipline

We are so busy with our work and family life that we often neglect to take advantage of the great wisdom in our scriptures. A spiritual life means different things to different people, of course. In one instance, for example, it may consist of the following regular practice:

- Taking at least five minutes of morning meditation before starting the day. If possible, another five minutes before retiring to bed can calm the mind and help with a good night's sleep.
- Spending a few minutes in prayer before beginning the day's activities. This surrender to the will of God helps to remain calm and handle whatever may be in store for us.
- Leading an ethical business life in line with your beliefs, so that your conscience is always clear.
- Using your spare time to read a scriptural book of your

choice or an uplifting book that helps restore your faith in your fellow human beings.

Self-discipline is learned through alert living. Alert living means being aware of your mind's functioning, rather than simply letting your mind control you. For example, alert living would encourage you to do the following:

- Before you speak, determine if what you wish to say is necessary, is beneficial, and will not cause harm.
- Examine your thoughts to see if you tend to dwell in the past or try to calculate the future.
- Learn mindfulness so you may live in the present. Meditation can help you with this.
- Watch that you are not postponing what needs to be done. Procrastination is the enemy of self-discipline.

Self-discipline requires that we control our five senses, which allow us to interact with the world.

Tongue, which is responsible for speech and taste. It is perhaps the toughest sense organ to control, and self-discipline serves to control what you say and what you eat. Controlling your tongue can help you stay healthy by eating healthy food. In addition, controlling your tongue by being alert to your speech means you need not regret what you say and can take time to weigh the impact of your words on a listener.

Eyes, which are responsible for us to interact visually with the world. It gives us direct optical knowledge of the beauty of nature and helps us understand the body language of the person we are talking to. However, moderation (self-discipline) in watching television and indulging in other leisure-time entertainment will give us more time for reading good books, including spiritual teachings.

Ears, which help us hear the external world. Using the ears to listen not to gossip but rather to excellent music and enriching discussions can help us improve our lives. Not abusing our ears with loud music and avoiding other excessive noise supports our health and allows our minds to focus on higher priorities.

Controlling your mind through the senses *can* help you maintain self-discipline and remain tranquil.

5. Practice Forbearance and Anger Management

For our purposes, forbearance refers to the attribute of self-restraint even when being provoked by another. It can result in an act of patience that may solve many of our problems in dealing with others. Forbearance will help you minimize the circumstances when you get angry and help you manage your anger so that it does not hurt anyone.

Forbearance can also mean being patient when facing some physical or emotional pain, instead of blaming others or yourself for the pain you face. This characteristic is exhibited by monks and others who have given their lives to the service of others. The value of forbearance can help you maintain happiness even under the most trying circumstances and learn to accept whatever life brings you. Once you develop this trait, you can face life's challenges with strength rather than despair.

As you may imagine, forbearance is a difficult characteristic to develop in our modern culture. Here, however, the interconnectedness of the values we're embracing become evident and supportive. Developing spirituality in your life is one practice that can help you develop forbearance. With it come the beginnings of self-discipline, which can be further advanced through alert living, so that you are aware of your behavior at all times. Regular meditation contributes to forbearance as well. Peace of mind at all times is the biggest benefit of developing forbearance.

The practice of nonviolence in thought, word, and deed—a considerable undertaking—goes far toward strengthening forbearance. Mahatma Gandhi, the leader of the nonviolence movement in India, practiced this throughout his life. (His biography is provided in essay 6.) Since all action starts in the mind, your thought should not contain any hints of violence to others, including animals. Thoughts become words, and if your thought is nonviolent, your words will not hurt anyone. If we are nonviolent in thought and word, it is impossible to hurt anyone through your actions. It takes considerable alertness to monitor your thoughts and avoid any violence in your thought. Replacing with love any thought that seeks to hurt anyone is the key to harmonious relationships. In theory, it can make the whole world calm and peaceful. What a noble pursuit to make it so!

Anger is potentially in everyone, but how you handle it speaks volumes about how much you value this value. You can process the anger in your mind and make sure your anger never hurts anyone. Anger can be expressed in a constructive manner so that the person who made you angry understands what he or she did and does not repeat the action again. Creating some distance between your anger and how you express it will help you in your maturity while helping the person with whom you got angry. Let's see how this constructive expression and created distance might be accomplished.

One of the primary reasons we get angry is when our desires go unfulfilled—a situation that can arise from any number of circumstances that we don't control. So when we feel the initial disappointment of an unfulfilled desire, and the earliest stirrings of anger, that moment is the time to analyze the desire itself to see if it was appropriate, and to understand the circumstances that led to your wish being unfulfilled. These steps, difficult as they are to take at first, are key to objectifying your anger by creating distance between its cause and circumstances and yourself.

To paraphrase the Bhagavad Gita, anger, if not controlled, can lead to loss of reason and delusion. And from delusion, you lose your discrimination and may perish. As news reports testify daily, many people kill others in a fit of anger and then spend their whole lives in prison, some of them in repentance. Anger is always destructive, and the amount of destruction typically depends on the level of anger. This emphasizes that learning to manage anger is a very important value and should be cultivated from a young age. Success in life—any sort of success in all kinds of lives—depends on learning to manage anger by practicing alertness.

In this competitive world, it's easy for complicated lives to be based largely on desires. That condition arises most often with the confusion between needs and wants. And wants are never satisfied in a bottomless economy, so they can turn into greed, as we discussed earlier. But a thorough analysis lets you work toward satisfying your needs and being careful about your wants. And this, in turn, helps short-circuit your anger when you face unfulfilled desires in other circumstances. When your wants diminish, forbearance and controlling anger become less difficult.

6. Look for Goodness in Others

For the most part, human beings yearn for peace and calm so that they can reach their full potential. Furthermore, everyone has within them a mixture of good and bad qualities. When we tend to focus on a person's negative qualities, we're likely being influenced by fear and anxiety. When we're inclined to see the goodness in others, we're more likely to learn to get along with many kinds of people from different backgrounds and cultures. This latter manner helps us remain calm and respond with openness and interest to new situations in our professional and personal lives, rather than reacting rudely.

Allowing a little time to process our thoughts helps us see the goodness in others. Something as simple as taking deep breaths for, say, 30 seconds before handling a stressful situation may help you to maintain your calm. Proceeding calmly allows you to then learn about the other party involved and, with interest, to see the goodness in them. Ultimately, you may find yourself willing to help them, rather than turning away from them as strangers. In my own life, I've interacted with people from many parts of the world and seen the goodness in people, irrespective of their nationality, color, culture, or professional background. I've made successful, lasting friendships that have enriched my life. And in my professional career of many years, I have encountered only two people who were not truthful and took advantage of my trusting nature. That's not a bad average!

Peace Pilgrim says in her book *Peace Pilgrim* (1982):

> In order to help usher in the golden age we must
> see the good in people. We must know it is there,
> no matter how deeply it may be buried. Yes, apathy
> is there and selfishness is there—but good is there
> also. It is not through judgment that the good can
> be reached, but through love and faith.

> Pure love is a willingness to give, without a
> thought of receiving anything in return. Love can
> save the world from nuclear destruction. *Love God:*
> turn to God with receptiveness and responsiveness.
> *Love your fellow human beings:* turn to them with
> friendliness and givingness.[2]

I've found that I see the goodness in people by staying cheerful and offering to help anyone I meet in any way I can. If you're kind and respectful, most people will reciprocate in a similar manner and their goodness will emerge. You'll bring out the best in them, and your relationship will be happy. This kind of interaction is essential to working for the common good and creating healthy communities. It's the basis of a successful democracy in which people trust others and help others with their time, talent, and treasure.

7. Don't Gossip

Too many of us unload our complaints about others behind their backs instead of confronting them and working out any misunderstandings. This can hurt another person in ways we do not and may never know. If the other person finds out from another source about what you've said, it will almost certainly create a broken relationship. At its very best, gossip is never productive. At its other extreme is malicious gossip, harmful to relationships and to the person whose spiteful purpose started the gossip. The rise of social media sites has made this kind of toxic hearsay quick and easy to disseminate,

2 Peace Pilgrim, "Living the Spiritual Life: The Power of Thought" in *Peace Pilgrim: Her Life and Work in Her Own Words.* (1982.) Free download, accessed July 29, 2024, https://www.peacepilgrim.org/.

so electronic rumormongering happens frequently and hurts many people, including many young people.

The Golden Rule would have you not speak ill of others since you would not want others to speak ill of you. So rather than resort to gossip, be courageous and speak directly to a person with whom you disagree. It may turn out that the person didn't understand you properly. It's always worthwhile to give the benefit of a doubt in dealing with people and never to assume the worst when you don't know the facts of a situation. Someone in a bad mood might have said something nasty and untrue about you. But if you're willing to talk to that person at a different time, tell them how they hurt you, and ask them why they said what they did, they may very well apologize and things can be settled and return to normal. As a corollary to abstaining from gossip, we need to understand that everyone is entitled to their feelings and work hard not to interpret anyone else's feelings from our own viewpoint.

8. Abstain from Jealousy

Jealousy arises largely from a lack of self-esteem. It differs from envy in that jealousy makes you feel threatened or fearful of losing your position or situation to someone else, whereas envy is the painful feeling of wanting what someone else has, such as possessions or attributes. Jealousy is a highly negative emotion that saps your mental energies and can lead to vengeance. Vengeance can lead to committing violence on another human being, and thence to a lot of trouble with the law. Mahatma Gandhi famously said, "An eye for an eye ends up making the whole world blind." So practice tolerance of the views of others on any topic of discussion. Developing a tolerant attitude overall will help keep you from feeling threatened by other people's ideas and opinions.

And this, in turn, can head off jealousy and vengeance, and channel you toward a tranquil life.

Everyone in this world is unique and has something to offer to society. With this knowledge, you can develop a strong sense of self-esteem, which will allow you to encounter other people without feeling anxious or inadequate. Self-esteem lets you feel content with yourself rather than threatened by someone else. It's also helpful to remember that things are constantly changing, and the person you may be jealous of one moment might have their own situation change, or your situation could change for the better with your self-effort. What's more, building up self-confidence by cultivating relationships with people who support and understand you is an important step toward avoiding jealousy.

9. Cultivate Resilience

Most successful people reflect resilience and rebound after a setback in their lives. The word *resilience* actually refers to two aspects of recovery: *strength* (hence the synonym *fortitude*) and *flexibility* (adaptability, suppleness). Both aspects are relevant to our consideration of this value. Resilience helps you in reenergizing yourself after a setback in your career and helps you develop the "can-do" attitude. Whenever I face a situation, I take time to absorb the situation and analyze what I could have done better. Then, instead of wasting mental energy by dwelling on the situation, I move ahead and see what I can do to improve it. A personal story will help illustrate this.

I was asked by a company in Canada to move there early in my career with the promise that I would be transferred to Denver as head of that office in six months. However, the economy crashed during that time, and the company decided to close its Denver office, telling me that if I became an immigrant in Canada, I could continue in the Canadian office. Considering the prospects for my wife and me, we decided we did not want to become permanent residents of Canada. Immediately, I called my friends in the U.S. and found out that a company I knew of in Chicago had an opening for a person with my qualifications. I called that company and flew to Chicago for an interview. They offered me a challenging position and wanted me to join them as soon as possible. I put my house up for sale in Canada and moved to Chicago within a week.

This move completely changed my career and life for the better, and I'm glad I moved quickly instead of blaming the situation and the company for breaking their promise. I accepted that things had changed, moved ahead with a positive attitude, and was able to rebound from the bad news of losing a job to the good news of getting a job I loved. So it's often in your hands to bounce back from an adverse situation, and blaming others or the circumstances will virtually never help. This lesson made me a stronger person, both emotionally and professionally. My belief is that every situation happens for the best, and with this, I look at the positive side of things and have never regretted any moment in my life.

An important habit that supports resilience is to analyze facts instead of being overcome by emotions when facing an adverse situation. If you do this, your mind works better and you may come up with solutions you never imagined. Negative emotions sap your mental energy, and your mind becomes your enemy instead of being your friend. Never let these emotions overcome you. If they come, just be aware of them and do something to cheer yourself up while you let the negativity disperse. In a proper frame of mind, you'll come up with the right approach to take, since the mind is capable of doing amazing things when you don't let it wallow in negativity.

Value for the Values

Many people profess values. But when it comes to living those values, some find excuses why certain situations just don't allow them to live those values. A strong commitment to the values we've been looking at will help us live these values on a daily basis—professionally and in interactions with friends and family. If the rule foremost in our minds and guiding all these values is to treat everyone as we would like to be treated, we will interact with others in such a way that we don't hurt them and are sensitive to their feelings. And as we increase the degree of alertness in our lives, we will be able to apply these values in all our thoughts, words, and actions.

Success in any business is based on trust. And if our customers, employees, and shareholders see that the values mentioned here are the foundation for a company, the company will succeed in the long term. In his book *Start with the Why*,[3] Simon Sinek gives numerous examples of companies that have become household names owing to the trust they built up by living the values with which they started the company. So in moving toward a life of tranquility, you'll want to place just as high a priority on cultivating the values you've embraced and living those values every day.

---

3 Simon Sinek, *Start with Why: How Great Leaders Inspire Everyone to Take Action* (Portfolio, 2011).

CELL-TIME MANAGEMENT

Instant communication in the digital age has brought new challenges in applying these values, especially with our cell phones constantly distracting us from the moment we wake up to the moment we go to sleep.

Under these circumstances, self-discipline and one of its components, alert living, can be invaluable aids in limiting our cell phone use. Here's a system I've used over the years so that I—and, in fact, our family—could spend more time together:

WEEKDAYS

- Cell phone **OFF** at home **until after breakfast**; check how the workday looked.

- Cell phone **ON during office hours.**

- Cell phone **ON after work for errands, in case of calls from home.**

- Cell phone **OFF upon arriving home for the day**; marks quality family time and relax, read, and recharge personal time.

- Cell phone **OFF during dinner time, applies to everyone**; per the famous saying "You are what you eat," and alert living means nutritious meals and eating moderate amounts, which in turn keep you physically healthy and mentally alert.

Many professionals have become virtual slaves to work—and, of course, their phones. This leads to more stress and health problems, and health mustn't be sacrificed to anything. Alert living cues us to how our thoughts, speech, and actions are responsible for our well-being. Alert living—that awareness of your mind's functioning—can help you control your cell phone use to make time daily for your family and friends and to renew yourself. You'll find you have time for exercise, reading, and listening to music—all activities that can help you stay healthy and be tranquil.

Having time for yourself allows you to reflect on whether and how you're following the values you've adopted, and to make as-needed adjustments to follow those values and build your tranquil life.

ESSAY 2

9 Steps to Tranquility

"We can create a more peaceful world by striving
for goodness in each moment, wherever we are."
— BISHOP DESMOND TUTU
speaking about the South African word *Ubuntu*

TRANQUILITY IS A QUALITY that a great many of us would love to have in these digital times, when we are surrounded by devices that distract us from anything remotely like tranquility. From the cell phone to our computer to the streaming shows on television, we have many things that take our mind away from being calm and peaceful. This essay will develop in detail the 9 Steps to a tranquil life, and my hope is that you will reflect on these steps and make the effort to practice them on a daily basis until your mind, which is conditioned by all its past habits, can outgrow those past habits and adopt these 9 Steps into your life.

The mental conditioning that happens at home and school until we finish high school has a strong bearing on the behavior we follow as adults. If you're told that achieving academic success is critical to doing well in life and earning a good income, you'll focus on that while not spending enough time on the interpersonal skills and empathy that are needed to be a good citizen of your community. The value placed on money and fame during your adolescent years has a bearing on the thinking you develop as an adult. I was told when growing up that following moral values is extremely important irrespective of the hardships it may entail. I was told at home by my parents and grandparents that helping other human beings is important, and my father specifically told me when I was in high school that setting aside at least 2 percent of my income to help others is very important. He suggested that as my earning ability increased, I could do more, but never to forget the 2 percent rule. These values have framed my life and have given me a lot of happiness and tranquility.

Humans are born with the desire to be happy and tranquil. The soul, the consciousness in us, is described as Sat-Chit-Ananda in the Hindu scriptures. Sat means we have goodness in us and also represents our faith in God, the Creator, who runs this universe. Chit is our consciousness, which survives the body, and Ananda is absolute happiness, which is with us always. So we are tranquil by nature, and during the period of growing to adulthood, we develop a series of strong likes and dislikes, which adversely impact our tranquility.

We forget the happiness we enjoyed as a child in our mother's lap and start reacting to our likes and dislikes, becoming happy when we get what we like and growing depressed when we have to face dislikes or disappointments in life. When a strong like is not fulfilled, we get frustrated and irritable. Dwelling on this further, we get angry at the people or situations that stood in the way of fulfilling our likes. This disturbs our tranquility, and we become stressed and unhappy.

The key to maintaining tranquility is the ability to manage our likes and dislikes and make them our guiding preferences instead of rigid absolutes in our head. All spiritual paths teach us how to manage these likes and dislikes. The only way to conquer our likes and dislikes is to stay objective under all circumstances. Analyze the facts without complicating them with your likes and dislikes.

One of the easiest ways to understand objectivity is to use the newspaper's obituary column. There, you can read of the deaths of so many people in the community, but you are not affected since you know that death is a fact of life. However, if it is someone dear to you, you become subjective and are shattered and ask yourself why it had to happen. You lose your tranquility for many days, and if it is your parent or spouse or child, waves of guilt might come over you if you have not done everything you could do for them when they were alive. Swami Dayanand Saraswati, a well-known spiritual teacher in the U.S. and India, has said, "Only when you see yourself from your capacity to manage your likes and dislikes, can you be successful." The success referred to here applies to all life situations, not just professional success. This ability to manage your likes and dislikes and be objective comes only with alert living, which means having the capacity to monitor your thoughts, words, and actions constantly. Such alert living will ensure tranquility and happiness. The mind will learn to look inward for happiness instead of hankering after the innumerable temptations that are always ready to take our mind away from being tranquil.

Our life is a variety of experiences, and if we learn from these experiences, we will be happy. Failure and success are just labels we put on our experiences and are two sides of one coin. Most successful people are those who learn from failures and know how to bounce back. Swami Dayanand Saraswati has said: "The beginning of spirituality is not blaming anything—not the Lord, not the world, not others and not oneself—it is readiness to address one's problems." Objective analysis of our problems is the first step to take among remedial measures to address our problems to the best of our ability. When we do this consistently, we gain greater self-confidence and tranquility. Our mental energy is not dissipated but focused like a laser on what can be done to address our problems. Once we do this, mental conflicts do not arise, and we are stress-free. A great way to feel good at the end of each day is to do what has to be done that day and not postpone it for another day. This requires a lot of discipline, which is discussed as the first step to gain tranquility.

A major cause of stress is an inflated ego, due to believing your success is all a result of your own effort. You must understand, however, that a lot is given to us from society, our parents, our teachers, and many people on the team we work with. Acknowledging all this support and feeling grateful reduces our ego, and we are thankful for our success but do not become proud. Also, the results from your work are not completely under your control and depend as well on the grace of God and many other factors that you do not control. Accepting the results and not expecting things that are unrealistic will greatly reduce the stress.

The best way to control your ego is to remain objective. This, too, assists you in analyzing situations without imposing your subjectivity. You can better examine your faults and improve. You can be aware of the contributions of others to your success and thank them, which will win you more friends, who may continue to help you as needed. A tranquil mind sees the world as it is: a beautiful creation of God. It allows you to appreciate the world and the people around you as they are, without expecting them to change to fit your likes and dislikes.

Cultivate Discipline

Self-discipline can be defined as training yourself to obey a code of behavior that leads to your goal. In his book *12 Rules for Life: An Antidote to Chaos,*[4] Dr. Jordan B. Peterson states in his Rule 2: "Treat yourself like someone you are responsible for helping." This important rule leads to helping yourself through self-discipline. You should take care of, help, and be good to yourself the same way you would take care of, help, and be good to someone you love and value. He states that "You have a spark of divine in you, which belongs not to you, but to God. We are, after all—according to Genesis—made in His image. We have the semi-divine capacity for consciousness." This gives us fortitude and perseverance, the essential ingredients of self-discipline.

Self-discipline requires you to consider what is truly good for you and not just what you want. This means forgoing temporary, instant happiness in favor of what is good for your health and mental well-being. It is similar to saying no to a child who wants to eat a handful of chocolates and skip a nutritious meal. As an adult, you would divert the child's attention and incentivize the child to eat the nutritious meal so he or she can grow up strong and healthy. You have to discipline the inner child in you whenever temptations to overindulge in eating or drinking try to take over. Similarly, you have to forgo the immediate happiness of buying things you cannot afford and falling into credit card debt, which, without you noticing, can creep into thousands of dollars. Mahatma Gandhi said, "He who is

---

4 Jordan B. Peterson, *12 Rules for Life—An Antidote to Chaos* (Random House Canada, 2018).

discontented, however much he possesses, becomes a slave to his desires. And really there is no slavery equal to that of his or her desires."

The Hindu sacred scripture known as the Bhagavad Gita states in chapter 6, verse 6, "For him who has conquered his [lower] self by the [higher] self, his self is a friend; but for him who has not conquered his self, his self is an enemy." We become our own worst enemy by giving control of our mind to other people, situations, or things. We human beings have been given free will to use our mind to discriminate between what is good for us and what is bad for us, and to choose good over bad. If you give up this precious attribute of the human mind by falling under the spell of the latest gadget being marketed, or surrendering to situations that will give you immediate pleasure but in the long run will be harmful, you fall into a downward spiral that may kill you or harm you significantly. Instances of drug overdose or alcohol abuse or over-indulgence in other substances that endanger your mental or physical health are all due to lack of self-discipline. So the step of self-discipline is the first step on your way to being a tranquil person who enjoys life, and who helps others enjoy life to the fullest.

The four pillars of Hinduism start with Dharma, or proper behavior to others in society as well as yourself. Dharma is the basis for whatever you pursue, whether it be the desire for health, wealth, or happiness. Self-discipline is essential to follow the rules of Dharma. Plato called it "the good." Dr. Jordan Peterson says, "Obedience is not enough. But it's at least a start (and we have forgotten this): you cannot aim yourself at anything if you are completely undisciplined and untutored. You will not know what to target, and you won't fly straight, even if you some-how get the aim right. And then you will conclude, 'there is nothing to aim for.' And then you will be lost."

According to the Bhagavad Gita, there are three types of mental tendencies in humans. These are:

- Noble and selfless
- Ambitious with a lot of selfish desires
- Indifferent with no sense of right and wrong

Developing and staying with the noble tendency requires you to practice self-discipline. This tendency helps you live a values-based life and naturally leads to tranquility, since it does not produce conflicting desires in you and your conscience is always clear. You do what has to be done, you stay objective in all situations, and you do not let the emotions of love and hate dominate your mind. You do what is right, and fulfill your responsibilities to yourself, your family, and your community. This tendency leads to both material and spiritual success, and you are happy to be with yourself, the source of all happiness. This happiness is not disturbed by anything that is happening around you. You stay calm under all circumstances and are also a source of joy to others. You have compassion for others and are sensitive to their feelings and needs.

Ambitious tendencies are dominated by your likes and dislikes, and by greed, anger, and mostly thinking about yourself. This tendency leads to mental turmoil, as you swing from happiness (when you get what you want) to sorrow (when you don't get what you want) and back again. It doesn't accommodate other points of view; instead, you become intolerant of others and are judgmental. All this is obviously not conducive to tranquility. You hold grudges and are driven by petty jealousies when your colleagues achieve any degree of success, such as a promotion that you thought you deserved. You are very subjective and are emotionally affected by situations beyond your control. All this is detrimental to your physical and mental health, and it makes it impossible for you to reach your full potential.

WHAT DOES SACRIFICE LOOK LIKE?

At a young age, I was taught to adopt noble thinking, and it has become easier to practice over the years. I learned from my parents that getting up at a regular time and going to sleep at a regular time helps develop discipline. So even today, I rise at around 5:00 a.m. every day (perhaps a little later on some weekends) and finish my prayers before I start my day. I take inspiration from daily prayer and surrender all the results of my work to God. This keeps me humble and enables me to work with others, giving them credit for their work and building a strong team. I sleep by 10:00 p.m. so that I can start my next day well rested. This discipline, developed in my school days, has helped throughout my life.

I chose to continue my education for a stretch of 21 years, going straight through college to get my PhD, instead of stopping at a bachelor's or master's degree. This decision opened many options for me, and I have lived a fulfilled life and done many interesting things around the world. At this writing, I am 76 years of age and am able to share my knowledge through teaching others while also fully enjoying my retirement. All this, too, required considerable self-discipline and sacrifice, especially in the initial years, but it paid rich dividends in the long run.

Whenever I have the opportunity, I urge young people to think long-term. My counsel is that it's never too late to get a good education and increase their options for a happy and fulfilled life.

Indifferent tendencies are dominated by slothfulness and not being motivated to perform at your best. You tend to procrastinate or to take shortcuts that will lead you to regret your actions later. You are hurtful to others and insensitive to their needs since you are not alert to them.

You are prone to revenge and take from society without a thought of giving back. You are deluded into wrong thinking and make bad judgments. You are careless and make obvious mistakes that can be costly in your life, whether immediately or eventually. Indifferent people are unhappy and complain about virtually everything, feeling that they're never dealt fairly by society. They look for entitlements without having a sense of responsibility for themselves or their loved ones. Their actions do not produce short-term or long-term happiness, and they simply wander through life without a sense of purpose.

All of us have a mixture of these three tendencies, and it's up to us to maximize noble tendencies and minimize ambitious and indifferent tendencies. Such an effort is worthwhile, and although it might not give short-term happiness or sensual satisfaction, it will provide tranquility and a peaceful life. God has given us the free will to use our mind to be our best friend and move toward noble tendencies and avoid ambitious and indifferent tendencies through alert living. But our free will is a powerful gift and must be cultivated with self-discipline. Thus it is the first step in the 9 Steps described in this essay.

Self-discipline requires sacrifice and delayed gratification. Jordan Peterson says, "Pursue what is meaningful, not what is expedient. Sacrifice means something better might be attained in the future by giving up something of value in the present." He says further, "It takes discipline to do this. Larger sacrifices are needed to achieve higher goals." Education for a brighter future and fulfilling life requires significant sacrifice. He mentions the life of the Greek philosopher Socrates, who made the ultimate sacrifice for the ultimate prize. When Socrates was accused falsely by the City of Athens for his beliefs, he did not take the easy way out. "His accusers provided him with plenty of opportunity to simply leave and avoid trouble. But the great sage had already considered and rejected this course of action." He listened to his inner voice—conscience—and accepted death by drinking poison. Twenty-five hundred years later, we still remember his decision and take comfort from it. Peterson continues, "He came to understand all that was happening to him as a gift from the gods." In Hindu theology, this attitude is called Prasada Buddhi.

Be True to Yourself

You have to honor and respect yourself. Without this, you cannot expect others to respect you. Being true to yourself helps you do what has to be done and allows you to live a life of no regrets. Speaking the truth and being ethical in your dealings with others helps in being true to yourself. Having a routine that helps you stay healthy and focused on your daily tasks will also help. This includes doing everything in moderation, ensuring you eat right (nutritious meals) and get enough sleep. Plan your day and stay with the plan without procrastination.

The best way of being true to yourself is to place a high significance on the values that are described in essay 1. Jordan Peterson cites the life of Socrates as the person who was always true to himself. He says that we can learn from the life of Socrates that "if you cease to utter falsehoods and live according to the dictates of your conscience, you can maintain your nobility, even when facing the ultimate threats; if you abide, truthfully and courageously, by the highest of ideals, you will be provided with more security and strength than will be offered by any short-sighted concentration on your own safety; if you live properly, fully, you can discover meaning so profound that it protects you even from the fear of death." Peterson goes on to say that "taking the easy way out or telling the truth—those are not merely two different choices. They are different pathways through life. They are utterly different ways of existing."

When I read the life stories of such people as Socrates and Gandhi, I wonder how far we have strayed from them in the 21st century, when most politicians and leaders are worried only about staying in power while being untrue to themselves. They will change their position on issues completely and adopt the currently popular position despite having a record of being opposed to that position in the past. Such politicians never feel bad about changing their long-held values and simply prostitute themselves to stay in power. As Peterson so aptly puts it, staying true to your conscience is the only way to ensure your long-term security and tranquility.

When you tell the truth, you don't have to remember what you told someone in the past, since your story will never change. There is an old saying in India: "People who lie have to say a thousand lies to cover up the original lie." A clear conscience ensures a tranquil mind, and nothing ensures a clear conscience than always speaking the truth. The Hindu scriptures have an apt phrase: "Satyameva Jayate," meaning that "only Truth wins always." This is adopted in the Indian national banner and was the guiding principle of Mahatma Gandhi, India's principal freedom fighter. In his classic book, *The Story of My Experiments with Truth*,[5] Gandhi speaks of the many struggles in his life to always speak the truth under all circumstances. In the collection *Mahatma*,[6] he is quoted as saying, "For me, truth is the sovereign principle, which includes numerous other principles. This truth is

---

5 Mohandas Karamchand Gandhi, *The Story of My Experiments with Truth* (Navajivan Press, 1927).
6 Meghshyam T. Ajgaonkar, *Mahatma: A Golden Treasury of Wisdom, Thoughts & Glimpses of Life* (India Printing Works, 1995).

not only truthfulness in word, but truthfulness in thought also, and not only the relative truth of our conception but the Absolute Truth, the Eternal Principle, that is God. In the march towards truth, anger, selfishness, hatred, etc. naturally give way, for otherwise truth will be impossible to attain." This says very aptly why being true to yourself is the best way to attain a tranquil mind.

The world will be a heaven on earth if everyone tries to always speak the truth and is transparent in their dealings with other human beings. I had many opportunities to make money in my business by not telling the truth, but I rejected all of them because a good night's sleep is more important to me than getting more money. Once a lie is exposed, there are severe consequences, including losing your freedom. The classic example that should remind all of us to speak the truth always is that of Bernie Madoff, the investment firm founder in New York City, who was exposed by his own family and died in jail serving a long prison term. He made his millions by cheating innocent investors, and once his scheme was exposed, he hung his head in shame and paid for his misdeeds. The United States makes perjury—that is, lying under oath—a crime with severe consequences. This is because the validity and smooth running of a society is dangerously impacted by people not speaking the truth and dealing with others dishonestly. Human greed, being the insatiable desire for worldly things, always forces one to betray oneself and, in turn, betray the fabric of society.

In my career, I started businesses in the U.S. and India and achieved a lot of my dreams. In dealing with business partners, my only message to them was "Say what you mean and mean what you say, then we will have a long-term successful relationship." Some people did not do this, and I had to make painful decisions about dropping them as business partners, although they had helped me in starting my business. One person had the habit of speaking outlandish lies about business prospects that he could bring to the company, and my friends and I spent a lot of time chasing these business prospects. After two years of doing this, I realized that he was untrustworthy and just dissolved the business. He hurt not only himself but the greater cause of helping the Palestinian people that he told me he was trying to accomplish with his connections in the Middle East. I have met some excellent people in doing business, and one person became like my brother and we remained good friends. So not being true to yourself hurts you and leaves the people you do business with, with a sense of deceit. In the long run, the only sure way to success in life and maintaining tranquility is to be true to yourself.

Tranquility requires a mind that is free of conflict, and speaking the truth makes you fearless and avoids mental conflicts with people you deal with. Alignment of thought, word, and deed is an important requirement in being true to yourself. The people you deal with will develop a high level of respect for you when they know you are a person who always speaks the truth and is honest in all personal relations. Jordan Peterson says that "if you betray yourself, if you say untrue things, if you act out a lie, you weaken your character. If you have a weak character, then adversity will mow you down when it appears, as it will, inevitably. You will hide, and there will be no place left to hide. And then you will find yourself doing terrible things." This is truly a bleak picture he paints for one who does not tell the truth and face the consequences. It is very important to analyze situations and never take the shortcut of lying when you could have told the truth and lived with self-esteem and pride. No short-term gain is worth the future of living in fear and shame because your lie could be exposed at any time.

A strong character is built by having the self-discipline to do the right thing, and the first right thing a person can do it is to be true to himself. Many people lie for simple things, and this just becomes a habit that then ruins their character. A good reputation and character will lead to long-term happiness and tranquility, and this is built by being true to yourself. Accepting whatever consequences might arise from telling the truth is a sign of emotional maturity. Victor Frankl, in his book *Man's Search for Meaning,*[7] says that "the way in which a man accepts his fate and all the suffering it entails, the way in which he takes up his cross, gives him ample opportunity—even under the most difficult circumstances—to add a deeper meaning to his life." Victor Frankl stayed true to himself under the horrible circumstances of a Nazi concentration camp and lived to tell the story of the atrocities dealt upon him. He is a symbol of the true meaning of one's life, which is preserving one's self-esteem and moral values under all circumstances.

The best way to be true to yourself is to practice alert living. Jordan Peterson says, "If you pay attention to what you do and say, you can learn to feel a state of internal division and weakness when you are misbehaving and misspeaking. It is an embodied sensation, not a thought. I experience an internal sensation of sinking and division, rather than solidity and strength, when I am incautious with my acts and words." This kind of close attention to your thoughts, words, and acts is cultivated deliberately over many years, and it pays rich dividends in living a life of tranquility. When thoughts, words, and action are aligned to

---

7 Viktor Frankl, *Man's Search for Meaning* (Beacon Press, 2006).

the truth, you have no fear. It could be a simple act of saying "I don't know" instead of making up things to please your listener. As Peterson fittingly puts it, "The better ambitions have to do with development of character and ability, rather than status and power."

Put Health First

"Health is wealth," an old adage says, and it's still true today when we live a stress-filled life and don't have enough time to eat properly and get enough sleep. You are what you put into your body and mind, so eating right and watching a minimum of television or video live-streaming will help you stay healthy. The content of what you watch and listen to is as important as the number of hours you spend in front of your computer or television screen. Reading the biographies of successful and tranquil people may help you develop ideas that you can implement into your own life. Along with eating right, daily exercise will help you stay healthy. In *Golden Giving*,[8] Keith Olson states that walking and bicycling are good, as is swimming, and yoga can help keep joints loose. A disciplined life incorporates daily exercise, and walking in fresh air in your local park can do wonders for your health and mental attitude. Other things Olson mentions include:

- Regular medical checkups
- Eating sensibly
- Not smoking
- Drinking moderately (if you drink at all)
- Keeping expenses in check and knowing your financial status

---

8 Vasudevan Rajamdan, Keith Olson, and Andrea Groner, *Golden Giving: Everything You Need to Know for an Enriched, Socially Conscious Retirement* (CreateSpace Independent Publishing Platform, 2017).

- Staying active and involved, mentally and spiritually
- Maintaining good relations with family and friends
- Having plans

Many books have been written about eating right, and a few pointers will be given here, since it is necessary for a healthy body and mind. Our body needs carbohydrates, proteins, fat, and vitamins. Guidance given by government agencies focuses on a balance of grains for carbohydrates; legumes, eggs, and meat for proteins; unsaturated fats; and fruits and vegetables. Instead of focusing on what to eat, I will focus on how regulating your eating patterns can keep you healthy. A regular breakfast and lunch at a given time and dinner a few hours before you go to sleep can help you stay you healthy. There are many guidelines on how much to eat and what constitutes a healthy breakfast, lunch, and dinner. The guideline I follow is to eat a breakfast of cereal and fruit, lunch consisting of carbohydrates and lentils, and a light dinner by 6:00 p.m. I always try to eat only between half to three-fourths of my capacity and leave room for water. Drinking about two liters of water per day is good. No soft drinks or drinks having calories.

There are five regions in the world—Okinawa, Japan; Sardinia, Italy; Nicoya, Costa Rica; Ikaria, Greece; and Loma Linda, California—termed Blue Zones by some,[9] where people purportedly live a longer, happier, and healthier life. These places share the following values:

- Maintaining a strong sense of purpose
- Eating mostly plant-based food
- Moving every day

---

9   Blue Zones, accessed July 25, 2024, https://www.bluezones.com/.

- Valuing low levels of stress, which naturally means restful sleep is a priority

Things they eat, drink, and do before bed for restful sleep are:

- Typically avoid foods with added sugar
- Drink green tea
- Drink red wine after 5:00 p.m. and in moderation
- Don't often eat right before bed
- Eat bread made from whole grains

The Bhagavad Gita mentions that eating, exercise, and sleep in moderation lead to a tranquil and healthy life. The Gita also prescribes types of food that lead to behavior characteristic of the noble, ambitious, or indifferent tendencies of mind mentioned earlier. Noble people like foods that promote longevity, intelligence, health, and cheerfulness. These foods are bland, substantial, and agreeable to the body. They are plant-based, have low sugar and salt, and aren't fried in oil or butter. The ambitious-tending people like foods that are bitter, acid, salty, very hot, and dry. They cause suffering (such as upset stomach), grief, and sickness. They also have a lot of processed ingredients and are tasty, but in the end, they cause health problems. Indifferent-minded people like stale, insipid, half-cooked, and unhealthy food. These foods consist of red meat, eggs, garlic, and onions. The food you eat has a direct bearing on your health. To be tranquil and healthy, therefore, we should focus on food that promotes noble living. As a bonus, current research has shown that this kind of food promotes a small carbon footprint on our planet.

The importance of putting health first was brought to my attention in my early forties when I was very busy running my company during the day, attending law school in the evening, and balancing all this with my family responsibilities. I became very sick one day while driving home from work, and I was lucky that my wife recognized something was wrong and rushed me to the emergency room. I had a major lung issue and needed surgery, resulting in several days of rest at home. This experience brought into relief the importance of putting health first. And since that time, I have developed a work-life balance and take time to eat right, get enough sleep, and never put work ahead of my health and family. The discipline of taking time to eat a healthy breakfast, a nutritious lunch, and dinner (having proteins, carbohydrates, and fat in the right proportions), as well as doing daily exercise, has kept me feeling young and energetic, even in my seventies. I have my annual physical checkups done without fail, take care of my oral health, and check with my ophthalmologist annually. Many young people think they are invincible and neglect their health while putting other priorities ahead of health. Unfortunately, they may suffer later with diseases that were preventable with regular health checkups and by following the advice given in this section.

Refine Your Attitude Toward Work

We all work to make a good living and have the dignity that comes from work and a career. Many people today are putting their goals of accumulating wealth and achieving professional status ahead of compassion, self-discipline, forbearance, and the other elements of a values-based life (essay 1). This change of focus makes them stressed, anxious, and harried, always trying to do more in a given day. My chosen path has been based on a very different philosophy, developed over a forty-four-year career in engineering consulting: to do the best I can every day and leave the results in God's hands. God has always given me what I deserved at the right time, and I have had a successful career, largely stress-free, while enjoying time with family and friends and taking time for vacations to enjoy nature. This attitude of doing your best every day and taking time to fulfill other aspects of life is a key ingredient to a tranquil and healthy life.

You have heard of many types of yoga, but the yoga that is stressed in Hinduism is Karma Yoga, detailed in several chapters in the Bhagavad Gita. The one verse that encapsulates the essence of Karma Yoga is in verse 47 of chapter 2, which states that your right is to work well but not to the results thereof. It also emphasizes that the fruits of action should not be your objective and inaction is not an option since you have to use your skills and education to make a living and serve society. The next verse states that giving up attachment to the fruits of your action and being even-minded in success and failure is called "Yoga."

What do these words mean in the 21st century, where things are very competitive and you are told right from childhood to get a good education so that you can earn a good living and be a successful person? It means that your full attention should be on doing whatever you do well (excellence being the goal) and that you should not be distracted by what the outcome of your work might be. There are many factors that determine the result of your work, of which you control only your effort and mental attitude. So it is foolhardy to set as your objective a result that you believe should receive. You strive to reach an objective but never give up if you meet failures along the way. The greatest president of the United States, Abraham Lincoln, failed in many of his attempts but never gave up till he reached his goal of maintaining the United States as one country, despite two factions that wanted vastly different things. After many failed attempts at seeking various public offices, he ultimately succeeded in becoming president.

Work provides us dignity and self-respect while providing a living. Many people focus on material goals and will do anything, even if it contradicts their ethical values, to obtain their goal. A good living is one that meets our needs instead of all our wants, which can be endless in the materialistic society in which we live. For some reason, people give respect to those with a lot of money and fame instead of those who serve society's needs through their work. Objects of such devotion include athletes, people in the business world, and Hollywood celebrities, while the hardworking doctor, teacher, or engineer garners little respect or recognition.

Once, my workplace circulated a survey in which people were asked if they would continue to work if they won a multimillion-dollar lottery. I answered that my work in the environmental cleanup industry was more important to me than the millions of dollars, and many were surprised. I felt a sense of purpose and accomplishment every day, and I would continue to be excited to work on my projects. This kind of attitude kept me happy and tranquil while meeting many frustrations in the progress of my environmental cleanups involving multiple parties. The long years it took to cleanup a contaminated property was a lot of fun since my attitude was one of service to society and gratefulness for the opportunities to serve.

One may consider work as a worship of God, who has given us everything through the natural bounties we enjoy. All work is a respectful offering to God, especially when you do it with that prayerful attitude. Then, your mind is fully focused on doing your work well and never worrying about the result that will ensue from your work. A story is told of two people who were working on the construction of a church, and one worker said, "My work involves hard labor each day, and I just do it to earn a living." The other worker was not mentally tired after each day's work, since his attitude was focused on building a beautiful church for God, which might take several years, and he was interested in doing his work and not on when it would be completed or how the church would look when it was done. There are several churches I have visited in Europe, including St. Peter's Basilica in the Vatican and Gaudi's famous church in Barcelona, and I marveled at the workers who have created such masterpieces for the enjoyment of future generations. Again, the attitude with which you approach your work can make it a joy and lead to tranquility, or you can frame it as a daily chore that has to be gotten through only so you can meet your wants.

Practice Daily Meditation/Quiet Time

Meditation is a time alone with oneself, where you shut out the external world and focus on controlling the mind, which is generally outward-looking. There are many groups around the world offering guided meditation and meditation techniques. But the process all begins with your determination to use meditation to calm your mind and make it tranquil. Without this determination to help yourself, all the lectures and books you read on meditation will not help you. Cell phone apps like Headspace offer messages to meditate upon. But unless used consistently and with the objective to calm the turbulent mind, these will be useless in your pursuit of tranquility.

The Art of Living,[10] a group started by Sri Sri Ravi Shankar (referred to as Sri Sri by his followers) in India many years ago, has chapters around the world to offer meditation classes to its followers. According to them, emotions carry us away from our natural state of being, which is to stay in the present moment and do the best we can. Instead, the mind wanders into the past, with regrets or pleasure, or into the future, with anxiety and worry being the result. The continuous bombardment of thoughts reduces our ability to think clearly, and we often end up reacting to the situation, instead of responding in an objective manner.

My teacher, Swami Tattvavidananda, defines meditation as "Being with oneself, and knowing all about oneself." When you take at least 15 minutes each day, and preferably twice a day, to meditate on yourself, you get to know the flow of your thoughts and can turn them inward to know yourself. It requires discipline to take the time away from the events of the day to spend time with yourself and reflect on the events of the day. By doing this, you attempt to control the reaction to the events instead of just reacting spontaneously and being affected by them, going through cycles of happiness or sorrow. When you meditate, you get in touch with the consciousness in you, the source of your being alive.

In common parlance, this can be called your conscience, and it helps you decide between right and wrong. When you meditate, you get to listen to your conscience amid the turbulent worldly thoughts that try to take control of your mind. This makes you have a clear conscience, and this leads to tranquility. Awareness in all you do is possible by watching your mind and giving space between the situation you are in and how you respond to it. This is also termed "mindfulness" by some experts,

---

10   For further information on the Art of Living, see https://www.artofliving.org/us-en, accessed July 26, 2024.

and many books have been written about being mindful in your daily life. By doing this consistently, you are the master of your mind instead of the mind distracting you from your goals in life.

Peace activist and spiritual teacher Peace Pilgrim has said that you get God's guidance when you are receptively silent.[11] Meditation is a way to be receptively silent when you shut your mind to other thoughts that are constantly swirling and let God's voice (your conscience) speak to you and guide you in your daily activities. A young friend who has chosen a life of service to others after her graduation as an engineer from a prestigious college in Canada told me recently that when she is working in the woods to help poor indigenous communities, she finds it very relaxing and the quietness of the woods helps her think clearly about life's priorities. So there are many ways of meditation, and you can choose what best works for you. The main idea is to quiet the thoughts that are always occupying your mind and find the inner peace that will help you relax and discover solutions to any problem you face in life. This daily habit of some quiet time for yourself helps you live a tranquil life.

Daily meditation and prayer in the morning and evening has been part of my life since my childhood and has helped me remain tranquil while pursuing my life goals. Although I had to struggle for a long time to get my PhD, I persisted without getting frustrated and finally got my degree. Even in my various career moves, which involved moving from the Midwest to the West Coast and back, and starting my own company and taking on several challenges, I remained tranquil, and I attribute this to my daily prayer and meditation. I also practice deep breathing

---

11   Peace Pilgrim, *Peace Pilgrim: Her Life and Work in Her Own Words* (Ocean Tree Books, 1982).

during my meditation sessions, which has helped my chronic asthma and to stay healthy in general.

There are many ways of improving your brain function, and these include eating right, getting sufficient sleep, and removing the negative thoughts that make your brain less effective. All this requires discipline, the first step mentioned in this essay. Meditation is a powerful tool in making your brain function better and be productive in whatever you do. It has been proved over millennia by the ancient rishis (spiritual leaders) of India, and there are many yogic practices that are available to improve your health, both physical and mental. Whatever practice you adopt, it is up to you to practice it regularly.

A turbulent mind filled with uncontrolled thought drains our energy, and we feel completely exhausted and frustrated. According to Sri Sri, "Meditation prepares the mind to calm down effortlessly and turn turbulence into tranquility. Meditation releases the stresses that are accumulated in our mind and leaves it fresh and clear. It brings the mind to the present moment which is the field of action. When we act with complete awareness of our action, when the mind is totally attentive to the moment, the action is perfect and mistakes do not happen." The tips to effective meditation, according to the Art of Living, is to choose a regular time every day, preferably in the morning, for meditation so that the mind can remain peaceful during the day. The steps involved are:

- Choose a quiet, comfortable place.
- Be consistent, with the best times being before starting the day in the morning and before going to sleep at night.
- Sit in an erect, comfortable posture, with your spine and head aligned and eyes gently closed.

- Make sure your stomach is neither full nor empty.
- Observe your thoughts and bring them to focus on a mantra given by your teacher. If they wander, bring them gently back to the mantra effortlessly.
- Do not be in a hurry; everything can be tackled well after calming your mind during meditation. Do it for at least 15 minutes at every sitting.

Group meditation might work for some people, but it is best to do it alone daily. I have practiced meditation for the last few years, and it helps me calm the mind and tackle the day cheerfully. If anything is bothering me, a few minutes of meditation brings everything into perspective, and I regain my composure. It has helped me be stress-free during my career and stay healthy, even with congenital asthma.

The Center for Healthy Minds at the University of Wisconsin-Madison, founded by Dr. Richard Davidson, has done extensive research into the benefits of meditation over several decades. They have studied the brains of Buddhist monks and have found direct correlations between their calm and peaceful demeanor and the years of meditation practiced by them. Dr. Davidson has been a longtime friend of the 14th Dalai Lama, and working with him and his monks, Dr. Davidson has studied the brain as it relates to meditation.

Dr. Davidson's research is broadly focused on the neural bases of emotion and emotional style, as well as methods to promote human flourishing, including meditation and related contemplative practices.[12] Davidson has long maintained his own daily meditation practice

---

12 "About Richard J. Davidson," Richard J. Davidson, accessed July 25, 2024, https://www.richardjdavidson.com/about.

and continues to communicate regularly with the Dalai Lama. He has introduced meditation to students on the University of Wisconsin campus.

Transcendental Meditation™ is a method advocated by Maharishi Mahesh Yogi, who has established a university in Fairfield, Iowa. The method encourages a restful state of mind beyond the surface level of your awareness. The Maharishi began teaching the method in India in the 1950s, it was popularized in the 1960s and 1970s, and it is now an international movement of meditators working to improve themselves. TM is a trademark and claims the following benefits:

- Stress relief
- Reduction of blood pressure, anxiety, depression, and anger
- Basis for a calm and peaceful life

Classes are taught by certified trainers over a period of four weeks, and the cost is based on ability to pay. The advocates of TM include many celebrities, and it is a systematic method of training the mind and achieving personal success and a calm demeanor.

David Henderson, senior pastor of Covenant Church in Indiana, in his book *Tranquility*,[13] describes the third rhythm—to become still and contemplate God. The first rhythm of rest is the daily cycle of wakefulness and sleep. The second is the weekly pattern of work and rest. The crucial third rhythm of rest, one we often neglect, is the routine cycle of engagement and disengagement, of forward motion followed by retreat into solitude and silence. Henderson says, "Getting still is a

---

13 David W. Henderson, *Tranquility: Cultivating a Quiet Soul in a Busy World* (Baker Books, 2015).

prerequisite to encountering God. 'Be still' must come before 'and I know that I am God' (Psalm 46:10). The more I'm on the move, the more occupied I become with motion itself." This scriptural citation indicates the importance of meditation in Christian teachings.

Swami Parthasarathy, an acclaimed exponent of Vedanta—a system of Hindu philosophy focusing on spiritual practices that lead to self-realization—says in his book *Vedanta Treatise*,[14] that "the mind of the modern generation is in a chaotic state. Its thoughts run wildly in all directions seeking pleasures of the world. … An agitated mind cannot concentrate. When you reduce your desires through spiritual practices, your thoughts no longer run helter-skelter. Your mind becomes calm and composed. It is more introvert. Such a mind can be brought to a single-pointed concentration by Japa or chant." Meditation is a technique to achieve this single-pointed concentration, and by doing this daily, you not only become tranquil but are better in your career and personal life. According to Swami Parthasarathy, meditation is nothing else but rising above desires. It helps you reflect on yourself and realize the futility of all the temporary pleasures that your mind dwells on and direct it to the higher consciousness within you, your soul, or Atma, in Hindu spirituality.

Build Work-Life Balance

In a 24-hour day, work occupies about one-third of the time, and the rest is for yourself and your family and friends. In today's hyperconnected society, you probably often take thoughts of work into other aspects of your life and may not be as effective a spouse, parent, friend, or citizen as you might otherwise be. In the worst-case scenario, you could

---

14   A. Parthasarathy, *Vedanta Treatise: The Eternities* (A. Parthasarathy, 2020).

end up lonely after your family and friends have left you, as you try to figure out why you spent so much of your life thinking about work and working for yourself or others and neglecting other aspects of your life.

Developing an effective work-life balance is an essential part of taking care of our health, both physical and mental (including spiritual), and of doing our duty with respect to our family and friends. Many people feel the urge to check their emails or social media even after coming home from work, but this behavior keeps the mind focused on externals, leaving no time to address exercise, eating right, or the state of important personal relationships. Humans are social animals and need the company of others, including family and friends, to feel fulfilled. If you neglect these relationships, your children can grow up not knowing much about you. And when they're adults and you want to spend time with them, you may find your kids just don't have time for you anymore. Similarly, relations with your spouse and friends can become strained, and you may regret your early years of busyness when, many years later, others around you have moved on with their lives.

Work does provide a sense of dignity and identity that's important to our self-image and role in society. Our work is a way of giving back to the society that has invested in our education and skill development. However, when other duties are neglected due to an overemphasis on work, we fail ourselves and society. The Hindu scriptures talk of the five responsibilities of every individual:

- Duty to our parents, who have nurtured us and provided for our basic needs
- Duty to our teachers and teaching institutions, who have given us a good education and made us into thinking adults

- Duty to fellow humans, who make up the society we live in
- Duty to the environment that nurtures us with valuable resources—food, water, earth, and air
- Duty to God, who has given us the values to live our lives fully

We fulfill our duties to parents by respecting them and taking care of them when they are old and need financial or physical help. We should find time to spend time with them during the year and seek their help in raising our children in a loving environment. This is especially important in today's world, with both parents working long hours to earn a living and provide the things our children need.

We fulfill our duties to our teachers and teaching institutions by getting involved with the university alumni association. By keeping in touch with our teachers and letting them know how our career progresses, we make them proud and happy. I've have found a lot of pleasure in giving my time, talent, and treasure to the institutions where I obtained my education. Over a 20-year period, my involvement with my college consisted of donating money for scholarships, arranging global reunions of alumni and the university, and mentoring young students. I was also privileged to give talks at the university to share my experiences with the students.

We fulfill our duties to fellow humans by giving to charity and sharing our time and talent with those who need our help. All religions stress the importance of charity and service to fellow human beings. We hear of inspiring individuals who take time to help others in need, especially after a natural disaster. I know an Americorps volunteer who went to New Orleans for several weeks to help the people affected by Katrina, a major hurricane that brought widespread death and property destruction to the city. There are many such unsung volunteers helping people who are affected by disaster or are simply struggling in their communities.

Unless you develop a good work-life balance, you cannot find time to volunteer in your community or time for your family. It has been important for me to spend a minimum of two hours per week during my career to help the those in need in the community and also to give to causes I believe in. In return, I've received immense joy and personal growth. Only because of work-life balance developed early in my career could I do this, and I feel blessed to have the opportunity to help others in my community.

We fulfill our duty to the environment by participating in cleanup of our rivers and parks and not polluting the air, water, or land. There are many fine organizations around the world and in every community that work hard to keep our environment clean and safe, and volunteering with such an organization is a way of fulfilling our duty. When we treat water with respect as a God-given resource to be shared with all, we will make efforts to conserve water and be mindful of the pollution of our water bodies.

Citizen advocacy for a clean environment is critical in a democracy, and time for this has to be taken out of our lives. All our laws and efforts to keep our environment clean have come out of citizen advocacy groups around the world. In the U.S., the League of Conservation Voters assures that citizens voice their concern for the environment and hold the government accountable through voter participation and year-round advocacy programs. Unless we have a well-developed work-life balance, we cannot fulfill the duties mentioned here.

We fulfill our duty to God by living a peaceful life and abiding by the moral guidelines He has provided. The principles of a values-based life build on the moral guidelines given in our scriptures, and if we live a life where we honor these values and abide by them, we are that much closer to building a harmonious society.

We've considered how a person working an office job can find the right work-life balance. Increasingly, however, people choose to work as independent contractors or consultants in their chosen profession from home, which allows them to work with a flexible schedule. If you choose such a setting, it is up to you to decide your priorities and fulfill all your roles in life without sacrificing time with family and friends in order to work long hours. The appropriate place for money and fame in your life still has to be decided by you, just as it does if you work in an office setting. And just as in the latter place, an imbalance between a desire for money and fame with the need for a fulfilled life with your family and friends can lead to grave regret later in life.

It's very possible to put these principles of a work-life balance into practice. My wife and I were committed to it, in fact. We both had demanding careers during which we brought up our daughter. My wife was a busy physician with a private practice, and I was an engineer who had to travel occasionally to project sites. Out of my career of 44 years, I had my own business for six years in Chicago and eight years in India. Despite all these claims on our time, we found time for each other and spent quality time with our daughter. Our desire for work-life balance allowed us to adjust our work schedules to accommodate our family needs and ensured that we stayed healthy while fulfilling our responsibilities at work. We found time to take vacations with our daughter to many parts of the world.

Many people these days continue to work well into their seventies and eighties, and a good work-life balance ensures that they are productive and enjoy what they do. "Burnout" doesn't happen when you've learned all along how to manage the work together with your other responsibilities in life.

Serve Others

I was taught at a young age that service to humanity is service to God. This has been an essential guiding principle in my life, and I have enjoyed the service opportunities provided during my life, both in the United States and in India. Douglas Alexander, international president of Lions Clubs International, says, "I grew up with the value that those who can help should do so. I was raised in Brooklyn, NYC, where most families worked hard and came home tired at the end of the day. But they saw the value in supporting one another. They knew that they were stronger together. And they knew that as tired as they were, or as steep as their own struggles seemed, they still had something to give and they did. It is so easy to make a difference." This spirit of giving permeates the two largest international organizations, founded in Chicago over a hundred years ago. They are Rotary International and Lions International, the latter of which I have been a proud member since 2006. These organizations work with Rotary and Lions clubs worldwide to provide millions of dollars in grants to make life better for those managing disasters or struggling because of hunger, disease, or other causes.

As Mr. Alexander puts it, "You don't have to end all suffering for humankind—not on your own. But you can ease one person's struggle. You can pick up their bag and carry it for a while." For us to do what Mr. Alexander urges us to do, we need compassion for our fellow human beings. In the book *Golden Giving: Everything You Need to Know for an*

Enriched, Socially Conscious Retirement,[15] the authors state that "for many, values come from religious teachings, and there are several clear guidelines to philanthropic giving set forth in religious texts."

Christianity stresses charity, and usually almsgiving is seen as about ten percent of one's income given back to the community. It also states that we may give our time unselfishly to our parents, spouse, children, and those in need. The Jewish faith stresses eight levels of giving, the highest of which is to help sustain a person before they become impoverished by offering a substantial gift, in a dignified manner, or by extending a suitable loan, or by helping them find employment or establish themselves in business so as to make it unnecessary for them to become dependent on others. Islam stresses charity as one of the pillars of their faith, and Muslims around the world give generously to help others in need. The Hindu faith stresses charity, sacrifice, and austerity as three values that should be practiced unflinchingly throughout one's life.

Serving others can be done in many ways, and finding what fits best is up to each individual. Most people usually give in one or more of three ways:

- They give their time to help others in need.
- They give their talent to an individual or organization in need of their help.
- They give their wealth to an organization of their choice.

All of us can give our time to those in need, as and when we see the opportunity to help. It could be a random act of kindness or a regular amount of time every week. For many years, I gave two hours

---

15   Rajaram et al., *Golden Giving.*

a week to a tutor-mentor program in Chicago, and it was very gratifying to see the children I worked with do well in school with the time we spent together every week. Giving your talents is easy, but you do have to find an organization or individual that can help place you to use your talents effectively. You can help a senior with your computer or cell phone skills so that they do not feel left out in this digital age. I enjoyed sharing my English language skills with several immigrants who were struggling to adjust to life in the U.S., helping them improve their speaking, reading, and writing.

Sharing your wealth may seem difficult when you are not earning a lot. But a Buddhist charity in Taiwan gives people a piggy bank in which they can save their coins and then return it to the charity once it is full. By doing this, the charity and its contributors have done amazing work helping many causes in Taiwan and around the world. My wife and I gradually increased our charitable giving from two percent when we started our careers to ten percent when our income increased substantially. I encourage all young people to give whatever they can from the start of their career so that it becomes a habit during their life.

The book *Golden Giving* features two chapters dedicated to giving, one to giving locally and one to giving internationally. The opportunities to give are available everywhere; you need only the will to look to find an opportunity that suits your beliefs and values in order to give regularly of your time, talent, and treasure. Volunteerism is popular in the United States, and the media emphasizes the inspiring stories of giving in their broadcasts, which encourages others to become volunteers in their communities. There are many unmet needs in communities that volunteers undertake every week, and they do this in part because the pleasure it gives them in serving others who need their help.

Since 1994, I've volunteered with the Greater Chicago Food Depository (GCFD), and I've been impressed by the number of volunteers who come every weekend to pack the food for Chicagoans in need. Recently, I was able to work with the Lions Club in Chicago and the Lions Clubs International to get a grant for $100,000 for the GCFD to buy blast chillers to store food and deliver it to the needy in Chicago. This is an example of one voluntary organization (Lions Clubs) to work with another voluntary organization (GCFD) to meet the needs of the hungry. Every year, about 800,000 hungry people are assisted by the food provided by the GCFD.

The Sikhs (adherents of Sikhism) believe strongly in serving others, and in their houses of worship, food is provided to the needy at all times by volunteers who gladly give of their time, talent, and treasure. In times of disaster, they mobilize these kitchens in the places where they are needed most to feed the hungry.

The least one person can provide to another in need is a kind word and any help they can offer with their time and talent. It reassures the person in need tremendously to know that a fellow human being is willing to help them and restores their confidence in themselves and in humanity. Especially when natural disasters strike, often unexpectedly, I am amazed at the number of volunteers and volunteer organizations that step in and stay there until the community rebounds. This shows that humans have an in-built capacity to serve others. But we often get caught up in our daily lives and do not use this capacity to the fullest extent possible. Volunteer organizations can mobilize this capacity in individuals, and the multiplier effect is amazing, as I have personally witnessed in the Lions Clubs International Foundation (www.lcif.org), Indo Universal Collaboration for Engineering Education (www.iucee.org), and Engineers Without

Borders USA (www.ewb-usa.org)—organizations that have given me and many others opportunities to serve those in need.

Volunteerism creates a sort of contagious sense of optimism simply in seeing other volunteers serve the needs of society. *Golden Giving* suggests a number of additional benefits of volunteer service, including:

- Bringing families closer when they participate together
- Meeting all kinds of amazing people, from donors to volunteers to the people in need
- Improved social and relationship skills
- Countering the effects of stress, anger, and anxiety, not least because you see people who have much less than you and yet are managing to live happily
- Increased self-confidence—doing good provides a natural sense of accomplishment
- A renewed sense of purpose
- The possibility of a longer life (Studies have shown that volunteers live longer because the good feeling they get from helping others contributes to a decrease in chronic pain and reduces the risk of heart disease and high blood pressure)

Live a Purposeful Life

Viktor Frankl, in his book cited earlier, *Man's Search for Meaning*, shows the limits to which one man can suffer while searching for meaning in his life. He survived many years of torture and forced labor by the Nazis in the Auschwitz concentration camp during World War II. Frankl approvingly quotes the words of Friedrich Nietzsche: "He who has a

Why to live for can bear almost any How." In his book, he describes poignantly those Nazi prisoners who gave up on life, who had lost all hope for a future and were inevitably the first to die. They died less from lack of food or medicine than from the lack of something to live for. By contrast, Frankl kept himself alive and kept hope alive by summoning up thoughts of his wife and the prospect of seeing her again, and by dreaming at one point of lecturing after the war about the psychological lessons to be learned from the Auschwitz experience. Rabbi Harold Kushner of Natick, Massachusetts, says in his foreword to the book, "My own congregational experience has shown me the truth of Frankl's insights. I have known successful businessmen who, upon retirement, lost all zest for life. Their work had given their lives meaning. Often it was the only thing that had given their life meaning and, without it, they spent day after day sitting at home, depressed, with nothing to do."

I have seen this happen in my own family. My brother-in-law was about to retire when he came to the U.S. for a visit, and in our conversations, he told me he did not know what he would do after retirement since he had focused his life on his work. I told him of the various possibilities and how my parents had found fulfillment in their retirement by helping others and their children whenever they needed it most. He was not much convinced and still worried. In the third week of his visit, he suffered a massive heart attack and died. His wife had to return with his ashes to India.

After many years of being active in various volunteer activities during my career and after my partial retirement, I decided to write a book to help others find purpose in their lives after retirement. I published the book *Golden Giving: Everything You Need to Know for an Enriched, Socially Conscious Retirement*. In it, I talked of the various ways one can serve others in their retirement years and find a renewed purpose in life. My co-authors and I shared our experiences in how we found happiness in service to others and how anyone can launch on a career of service after their professional career is over.

In his book, Frankl describes many instances of how he survived the torture of forced labor and inhuman living conditions at Auschwitz. He says, "I became disgusted with the state of affairs which compelled me, daily and hourly, to think only of such trivial things (What will be there to eat after a long day of hard labor?). I forced my thoughts to turn to another subject. Suddenly, I saw myself standing on the platform of a well-lit, warm and pleasant lecture room. In front of me sat an attentive audience on comfortable upholstered seats. I was giving a lecture on the psychology of the concentration camp! All that oppressed me at the moment became objective, seen and described from the remote viewpoint of science. By this method I succeeded somehow in rising above the situation, above the sufferings of the moment." This shows that our mind can take us to a place much different from our current difficult situation if we dream of a higher purpose that our life could have. As John Milton said in *Paradise Lost*, "The mind is its own place, and in itself, can make a Heaven of Hell, a Hell of Heaven."

Frankl further says that "the prisoner who had lost faith in the future—his future—was doomed. With his loss of belief in the future, he also lost his spiritual hold; he let himself decline and became subject to mental and physical decay. Usually this happened quite suddenly, in the form of a crisis, the symptoms of which were familiar to the experienced camp inmate. We all feared this moment—not for ourselves, which would have been pointless, but for our friends." This shows that having the hope of a brighter future is essential for our survival during difficult times. If we don't have a purpose in life that is higher than the current situation we are in, we lose hope soon. The Hindu scriptures tell us that Ultimate Freedom, called Moksha, is a higher purpose that all human beings can aspire to in this life. It tells us that in giving up selfish desires and having faith in the future that God has for us, we can all strive to become better every day and achieve Moksha, which means an end to this endless cycle of life and birth. (Hindus believe in the transmigration of the soul after death, leading to another birth based on the merits and demerits of the previous life.)

Always See the Big Picture

Many of us tend to get bogged down in whatever situation we're in at present, and instead, we worry about the future. I did this in my college years, wondering what would happen when I graduated and what kind of career I'd have. My faith in the scriptures told me that if I put in my best effort in college, things will be good in my professional career. With that faith, I handled every situation as it came along and didn't worry about the future. I learned to see the big picture of life and not get stuck in day-to-day events. As Richard Carlson put it in his book *Don't Sweat the Small Stuff . . . and It's All Small Stuff*,[16] there are simple ways to keep the little things from taking over.

I've seen many people who get so bogged down in their current situation that they can't realize all the blessings they have, and they get depressed. When this happens, I suggest that they visualize what could happen in the future, and together we look at how this future scenario can be managed if they approach it in a different way. I assure them that

---

16   Richard Carlson, *Don't Sweat the Small Stuff . . . and It's All Small Stuff: Simple Ways to Keep the Little Things from Taking Over Your Life* (Hachette Books, 2017).

change is one of life's constants, and the current situation can change in the next moment if only they have faith in themselves. Self-confidence is essential so that a person can step back and see the big picture, rather than simply standing in the middle of their present situation and being overwhelmed by events swirling around them.

The past is something we can do nothing about except by using it to learn from our experience. The future is unpredictable and not yet within our reach. So if we do our best at the present moment, success is assured. The present is a gift from God, and all we need to do, all we can do, is to put forth our best effort. Combining this effort with seeing the big picture of life allows us to live the present moment worry- and stress-free.

Every present situation is temporary: an episode within the big picture of life. And understanding this relationship can help you adjust your entire point of view and become objective. This ability is essential for developing emotional stability and holding on to happiness. The big picture also includes your family and friends, and when you seek their support during difficult times, life becomes manageable. We are not alone in this world; we are connected to our community. And this realization, too, helps us retain our optimism and see the big picture that life has for us, and remain happy through all situations.

I've always counted my blessings, and this has kept me happy in my career and unbothered by the small frustrations I come across during my workday. I just look at each day as a fresh opportunity to help others and do the best I can at work and at home. This approach to looking at the big picture of my life has kept me steady and content under circumstances that many people would have found distressing or perhaps even agonizing. I can testify, therefore, that viewing the big picture is virtually always preferable to detailing and bemoaning the minor problems we face in our daily interactions at home or work.

Summary

The 9 Steps laid out in this essay are all building blocks with which to live a tranquil life. As you work on each step, the other steps seem to become easier to achieve, and you will eventually reach the level at which you can remain tranquil for most of the day.

There is no correct sequence in which to achieve success in these steps. But the first step of self-discipline is the most important, without which it is hard to make progress on this journey. Once you reach a level of daily tranquility, you will see how your health and well-being improve and your attitude toward life becomes one of optimism and cheer.

There are many inspirational stories that you can read of people in the past who have achieved such tranquility under the most trying circumstances. There are also stories in the media of ordinary people doing extraordinary things to help their fellow human beings. I am struck by how people respond to others affected by a natural or man-made disaster, drop their own daily routines to step forward and help those in need. In the aftermath of the Katrina disaster on the Louisiana coast in 2005, I heard of many people who simply took off for a few months to help the poor who were severely impacted by the disastrous storm. Civic organizations immediately granted large sums of money, and local volunteers to stepped up to help the affected community. This is the resilience of the human spirit, and serving those in need conveys the double blessing of helping you reach a level of tranquility in your life and being a result of that tranquility once it is achieved.

ESSAY 3

The Scientific Basis for Tranquility

Yoga is a method for restraining the natural turbulence of thoughts,

which otherwise impartially prevent all men, of all lands, from glimpsing

their true nature of Spirit. Yoga cannot know a barrier of East and West

any more than does the healing and equitable light of the sun.

— PARAMAHANSA YOGANANDA

Indian American monk and guru

SCIENCE HAS ALWAYS BEEN interested in the mind, and neuroscientists and psychologists have long been learning about the mind and about how learning to control some of its workings can help us attain tranquility. The brain controls our body's hormones, nervous system, and immune system, among other structures and processes. Our emotions and thoughts, too, affect the brain. The mind and body both, when well maintained, help keep us healthy.

The mind is a multifaceted organism, and its health is critical to physical health. The mind-body connection has been studied by many scientists in Western countries. However, the spiritual basis for and observations of the mind-body connection have been ongoing in the Eastern cultures of the world for thousands of years. India, in particular, has contributed many and various ways to influence and control the mind, and these studies and systems have been disseminated throughout the world. In significant ways, therefore, major contributions to the science behind yoga and meditation were made by the philosophers and spiritual leaders of ancient India.

The mind is a mixture of consciousness and the brain's biochemical and genetic makeup. It is a flow of thoughts that arise and subside as we encounter situations during the day, together with past memories. Unless we learn to control and channel these thoughts in a positive direction beneficial to our health, we can end up in the midst of negativities that can directly affect our physical and mental health. And unless we learn to ignore the noise created by negative thoughts, we cannot achieve our goals in life. Yoga and meditation can help in this effort.

Yoga and Meditation

Yoga is an art and a science that leads to the union of mind and body. It focuses on the science of healthy living, the mind with the body and man with nature.[17] The science of yoga is believed to have originated thousands of years ago in India and aims to manifest self-realization and inner harmony. It is estimated that about 76 million people in the United States practice yoga, with a majority of them being in California and New York. The regular practice of yoga has both functional and structural effects on the brain, mainly through posture, motivation, and sensibility. Meditation is a self-directed mental process that connects thoughts, behavior, emotions, and perception and is a discipline perfected by the ancient rishis (philosopher-sages) of ancient India. It has been proven that yoga and meditation improve cognition and enhance the capacity of the body and mind to relax and get rid of stress.

---

17   "The Science Behind Yoga and Meditation," Indiguruji, December 12, 2020, Indifamily, https://www.indifamily.com/the-science-behind-yoga-and-meditation/.

The Isha Institute of Inner Science in Tennessee conducted a controlled experiment with 106 participants in April 2018.[18] The study was planned and implemented by Dr. Vijayendran Chandran of the University of Florida. For eight days, the participants ate a vegan diet, had consistent wake and sleep patterns, remained silent, and meditated for up to 10 hours every day. The results were extremely interesting.

Study participants' final blood samples showed that 220 genes had been activated that are involved with anti-inflammation response and with generating a strengthened immune system response. Blood samples were taken before and after the 10 days of meditation. The difference in the two samples indicated that effective nondrug treatment for immune-related conditions such as multiple sclerosis was possible and could produce lasting improvement on the health of individuals. The study concluded that even 20 minutes per day of regular meditation could be enough to activate these genes and might even serve as a treatment for Covid-19.

Studies and individual experience have shown that regular yoga and meditation can yield a large number of benefits, including:

- Relief from anxiety and depression and reduction of harmful inflammation
- Lower blood pressure by helping relax and widen blood vessels
- Improved sleep quality and spiritual well-being
- Reduction of chronic pain and improvement of physical well-being

---

18   Nick Keppler, "Scientists Unravel an Intriguing Link Between Meditation and Immunity," *Inverse*, January 17, 2022, https://www.inverse.com/mind-body/ meditation-boosts-immunity.

- Relief of migraine and improvement of lung capacity and mental concentration

Having practiced yoga and meditation, including regulated breathing (pranayama), for many years, I have experienced most of these benefits myself. For example, I was suffering from chronic asthma for some years, but now my asthma is well controlled and I am healthy and able to do all the things I want to do to achieve my life goals.

Neuroimaging techniques such as the fMRI, MRI, PET, and SPECT have revealed significant changes that yoga and meditation have produced in both brain shape and connectivity (that is, the strength of interactions between areas of the brain that process information). Many studies throughout the United States have demonstrated the impacts of regular meditation on the functioning of the brain and tranquility.

Scientific Studies of Meditation's Effect on Tranquility

Many people in the field of neuroscience have been interested in how our brain changes in response to meditation. Outstanding among such groups is one in Madison, Wisconsin, led by Dr. Richard J. Davidson, that has been consistently studying this subject for over four decades. Dr. Davidson and his colleagues have even had Buddhist monks come to the university in Madison and meditate for long hours to see how their brains register positive changes both during the process of meditation and as a result of long-term meditation. The team's efforts have been documented in the book *The Science of Meditation* by Dan Goleman and Richard Davidson, published in 2018, which provides the basis for the greater part of the substance in the following pages.[19] The book also summarizes much of the other research throughout the United States and is very revealing as to how the brain responds to meditation. One study, for example, showed how busy professionals who constantly complained of a lack of available time could, after a period of meditating regularly for 20 minutes a day, achieve some degree of tranquility.

In 1992, for the first time in a public meeting, Dr. Davidson proposed the concept of neuroplasticity as a way to resolve the battle between nature and nurture. Neuroplasticity, he explained, shows that repeated practice of mindfulness meditation (a technique that focuses on awareness of being in the moment) can change the brain by shaping it. He concluded that we therefore don't have to choose between nature and nurture, that they instead interact, each molding the other. According to Dr. Davidson, "[N]europlasticity provides an evidence-based framework and a language that makes sense in terms of current scientific thinking.... [It provides] a way of thinking about how intentional training of the mind, like meditation, might shape the brain."

Dr. Davidson proved scientifically what was stated by Lord Krishna in the Hindu scripture known as the Bhagavad Gita over 5,000 years ago: that constant practice can tame the turbulent mind (Gita, chapter 6, verses 35 and 36). Lord Krishna emphasized that excessive attachment to worldly objects of happiness must be given up and added to this regular practice (that is, meditation) in order to tame the mind and remain tranquil. If you can keep the mind resolved in yourself through meditation, instead of being restless and pursuing the innumerable desires within you, you have the opportunity to attain and maintain tranquility.

---

19   Daniel Goleman and Richard J. Davidson, *The Science of Meditation: How to Change Your Brain, Mind and Body* (Penguin Life, 2018).

Benefits of Mind Control

A mind free from disturbance has value in lessening human suffering, a goal shared by science and meditative paths alike. Dr. Davidson's colleague, Carol Ryff, posits a model of well-being with six arms:

- Self-acceptance, being positive about yourself
- Personal growth, or developing toward your full potential
- Autonomy, independence in thought and deed, free from social pressure
- Mastery, feeling competent to handle the complex modern world
- Satisfying relationships, with warmth, empathy, trust, and mutual concern for others
- Life purpose, with goals and beliefs that give you a sense of meaning and direction

Ryff sees these qualities as a modern version of Aristotle's "highest of all human good," the realization of your unique potential. These qualities contribute to overall tranquility in one's life.

Dr. Davidson's research has shown that meditation can help with stress-worsened diseases like diabetes and hypertension. Our brain has the ability to anticipate the future, and worry about it, as well as to think of the past—and regret it. He mentions experiments done at his laboratory and others in the United States in which meditation has helped patients with stress reduction and chronic pain. At the University of Massachusetts Medical Center in September 1979, for instance, Jon Kabat-Zinn started the Mindfulness-Based Stress Reduction (MBSR) program. He showed that by using the MBSR program, patients were able to uncouple the cognitive and emotional parts of their experience of pain from the pure sensation, a perceptual shift that was itself a significant relief.

Using his Zen Buddhist background and Vipassana (an Indian meditation technique), Jon taught a sitting meditation in which people pay careful attention to their breath, letting go of thought or sensations that arise. This is also similar to the Pranayama meditative yogic breathing technique taught widely in India that helps to improve lung function and overall health while also calming the mind. There are many variations of the Pranayama method, each modifying the inhalation and exhalation steps to produce various benefits. Pranayama is the method I've practiced since my childhood that has helped me control my chronic asthma and live a healthy, fulfilling life, as well as helping make me a tranquil person with an accepting point of view of what is happening in my life, instead of stressing myself with unreal expectations. In his own practice, Jon has extended his work to include mindful eating, walking, and general awareness of life's activities, including relationships.

The Mind and Life Institute, based in Charlottesville, Virginia, has been working with the Dalai Lama and Tibetan monks for many years. The institute developed and continued to refine the practice of Mindful Attention Training, which starts with a full focus on the breath, then progressively hones attention to observe the natural flow of the mind stream, and finally rests in the subtle awareness of awareness itself. Mindful attention training results in reduced amygdala activity in response to disturbing pictures. The amygdala is the brain's radar for threat: it receives immediate input from our senses, which it scans for safety or danger. If it perceives a threat, it triggers the brain's freeze-fight-or-flight response. The amygdala also responds to anything important to pay attention to, whether we like it or dislike it. The benefits of mindfulness can be obtained even with 20 minutes of meditation a day, within a week—that is, by anybody who has the discipline to do it regularly. The institute has also found that regular meditation may be able to mute our emotional response to pain and so make the pain bearable.

Results from Meditation Retreats

Goleman and Richardson have conducted many meditation retreats with selected participants in which they observed the participants and measured their brain functions. They reported on the results of their findings that may be summarized as follows:

- Participants could control their emotions well and refrain from acting on an impulse or whim.
- The states practiced in meditation gradually spill over into daily life to mold the meditator's personality traits, especially those involved in handling stress.
- The ability to manage stress (which depends upon the connectivity between the prefrontal cortex and the amygdala) will be greater in long-term meditators compared with those who have only done the MBSR training.
- The more hours of meditation practice, the more quickly the amygdala recovered from stress. Thus, one who practices meditation regularly has lessened stress reactivity and more resilience in handling life situations.

In their book's chapter "Lightness of Being," Goleman and Davidson emphasize that most of our stress comes from focusing on the difficulties of our relationships, our worries, and our anxieties. When we focus on challenging pursuits such as rock climbing or running a marathon, those internal anxieties take backstage in the mind. Similarly, if we get involved in volunteering and helping others in need, our mind becomes less self-focused and keeps us happy. I have found that throughout my life, when I count my blessings and focus on how I can be of help to others, I am grateful and stress-free. Meditation aims to make the relief from our self-obsession an ongoing fact of life.

Traditional meditative paths contrast our everyday mental states—streams of thoughts, many laden with anger, or even simply to-do lists that never end—with a state of being free of these weights. And each meditative path, in its own particular terms, sees lightening our "sense of self" as the key to our inner freedom. The sense of "mine" is evaporated, which is the essence of all spiritual practices: lightening the system that builds our feelings of "I," "me," and "mine."

Moksha, in the Hindu tradition, is roughly equivalent to salvation in Christianity, but its process involves the lightening of our sense of self and a focus on the source of all creation, God. Goleman and Davidson quote the Buddha, who likened the self to a chariot, a concept that arises when wheels, platform, yoke, and so on are put together but which does not exist save as these parts in combination. The chariot is you, your mind with the five senses is the horse held by reins, and your intellect is the driver of the chariot. As long as your intellect is focused on your goal of inner freedom, the mind and five senses take you to your goal and away from worldly worries and its innumerable desires.

Meditative traditions of all kinds share a common goal: letting go of the constant grasping—the stickiness of our thoughts, emotions, and impulses—that guides us through our days and lives. By doing this, we can focus on being at peace with ourselves and happy without the need for the temporary pleasures that the world constantly offers us. Some Christian theologians use the term *kenosis* for the emptying of the self, where our wants and needs diminish while our openness to the needs of others grows into compassion. And in Islam, as a Sufi teacher has put it, "When occupied with the self, you are separated from God. The way to God is but one step, the step out of yourself." Mind training lessens the activity of our "self." "Me" and "mine" lose their hypnotic power, our concerns become less burdensome, and we lighten our self.

Dr. Davidson has conducted numerous studies at the University of Wisconsin on the effects of meditation on the human brain. In one study, he had a control group of volunteers participate in meditation sessions along with seasoned meditators (those having some 4,200 hours of meditation practice). He told the combined groups that they would get money whenever they recognized certain geometric shapes within an array. This created a mini-attachment for the money. In a later phase, when he told everyone to simply focus on their breath and ignore those shapes, he found that the seasoned meditators were less distracted by the shapes than were the control group. This response also reflected, physiologically, that the seasoned meditators possessed decreased gray-matter volume in a key region of the brain, the nucleus accumbens. This was the only brain region that showed any changes compared with the brains of the control group. A smaller nucleus accumbens therefore apparently diminishes the connectivity between self-related brain regions and the other neural components that ordinarily function to create our sense of self.

This scientific study clearly bears a relationship to the observation in Hindu texts that show meditators achieve an ongoing compassion and bliss, but with no attachment to self. The Hindu texts describe a state of being called Vairagya, in which attachment drops away with the continue practice of meditation. Vairagya, or a sense of detachment, happens spontaneously rather than through force of will. With this shift emerges an alternative source of delight in sheer being. These seasoned meditators train themselves to be as mindful in their daily lives as during meditation sessions.

According to Dr. Davidson, meditators have lessened connectivity among other key areas for self-focused thought (such as the various nodes of default circuitry and the posterior cingulate cortex). With such change in the brain's connectivity and activity, the mind is truly beginning to settle and the self-narrative is much less sticky. Normally, we hash over thoughts and feelings (often unpleasant) that focus on ourselves. During mindfulness and loving-kindness meditation, there is a decrease in stickiness and the mind has a decreasing ability to hijack your attention. Scientific studies have shown that meditation allows you to focus less on yourself and make the mind available for things you want to achieve in life. The lightness of being brings about a lasting sense of happiness and reduces anxiety over things that are happening in your life. Even 20 minutes of daily meditation done over long periods of time can have significant impact on your level of fulfillment and happiness.

Meditation and Mental Disorders

In their book's chapter on "Meditation as Psychotherapy," Goleman and Davidson cite the work of Dr. Young of New York City and psychologist John Teasdale of the University of Oxford (with Zindel Segal and Mark Williams) in noting that among people suffering with depression so severe that drugs or even electroshock treatments were no help, the use of mindfulness-based cognition therapy (MBCT) cut the rate of relapse by half, more than any medication. Davidson and Goleman analyzed 47 studies on the application of meditation methods to treat patients with mental health problems, and the overall findings indicate that meditation can lead to decreases in depression (particularly severe depression), anxiety, and pain to about the same extent as medications can but without any side effects. Meditation also can, to a lesser degree, reduce the toll of psychological stress. Loving-kindness meditation may be particularly helpful to patients suffering from trauma, especially post-traumatic stress disorder (PTSD). A psychiatrist friend of mine gave up her practice and started teaching meditation to patients with mental illness, and she swears to the benefits of meditation. She believes that medications for mental health patients should be reduced and more meditation included in their treatment.

A Healthy Mind is a program started by Dr. Davidson at the University of Wisconsin–Madison. The program teaches meditation-based strategies to cultivate well-being specifically designed for people who don't have time available to set aside for meditation. It can be tailored to piggyback your practice on something you do anyway, such as commuting or cleaning the house. Since the main payoffs for meditation lie in how you handle everyday life, the chance to practice in the midst of life could be a strength. The program's digital platform is being studied by Dr. Davidson's team to determine the app's benefits. Already MBSR, Transcendental Meditation, and generic forms of mindfulness are in easy-to-access forms anyone can benefit from. The key to their benefit is that participants have the discipline to use one of them regularly, and see how it benefits them in handling stress and other life situations.

The World Health Organization defines health as including "complete physical, mental and social well-being." Health is *not* just the absence of disease or disability. Given this definition and the acknowledgement of the scientific efficacy of meditation and its beneficial effects, it is remarkable how little active support goes into improving attention in children. Considering the lengthy period of growth in the brain's circuitry that childhood offers, it's rather startling that no additional enhancement is available that might strengthen those circuits. Children are frequently diagnosed with attention deficit disorder (ADD) and given medications that can have significant side effects. The science involved with cultivating attention is quite robust, but it often seems that the educational system largely ignores this resource for cultivating not only attention but kindness, caring, compassion, self-regulation, and a capacity for human connection.

Just as we give attention to traditional academic skills such as reading and math, it is important that we expand what children learn to include crucial skills for living a fulfilled life. Dr. Davidson's work on neuroplasticity tells us that neural networks in brain circuitry can be guided in the best direction through training like the Kindness Curriculum. The Kindness Curriculum begins with very basic, age-appropriate mindfulness exercises. The children first listen to the sounds of a bell and pay attention to their breathing as they lie on their backs, small stones placed on their tummies rising and falling with each breath. They then use that mindful attention to focus awareness on their bodies, learning how to pay close attention to those feelings while interacting with other kids—particularly if another child has gotten upset. The children are encouraged to practice helping one another and to express gratitude. Dr. Davidson's team has developed a video game called *Tenacity*, which kids can play on their iPads. They have found that playing this game for just 20–30 minutes daily over two weeks results in increased connectivity between the brain's executive center in the prefrontal cortex and the circuitry for focused attention.

The work of Dr. Davidson and others in the United States has shown clearly that sustained mind training alters the brain both structurally and functionally: proof of concept for the neural basis of altered traits that Eastern practitioners have described in their texts for millennia. The amount of benefit is directly proportional to the effort we put in for daily meditation or other mind training. Dr. Davidson urges the adoption of this mental training on a grand scale—particularly kindness and compassion—in the hope that it will lead to changes for the better in our communities and ultimately in nations. He further suggests that this training will enhance our individual thriving as well as the odds for our species' survival. He is inspired by the vision of the Dalai Lama, with whom he has worked for many years, who says that all of us can do three things:

- Gain composure, or inner calm
- Adopt the moral rudder of compassion
- Act to better the world

Dr. Davidson emphasizes that each of these goals can be products of meditation practice. He suggests this as one solution to an urgent public health need: reducing greed, selfishness, us/them thinking, and impending eco-calamities, and promoting kindness, clarity, and calm. We can alter our collective mindset by focusing far more on the numerous acts of goodness that take place in society rather than on the negative things, which are usually what's heard on audio news and TV broadcasts. This opens up the possibility of inspiring people to do what they can to help others rather than focusing on their own problems and thus becoming more depressed.

Practicing meditation and working to help the poor in my community for the last 27 years has transformed my own life. Since retiring, I rise early every day and spend a few hours connecting people who are doing good work so that their impact can be magnified. With the availability of the internet, I'm able each week to teach young people in India about how they can improve the world and how they can work on present pictures of life's possibilities instead of getting bogged down by the daily setbacks life offers them. This keeps me connected with the energy of youth, and I am hopeful every day of things improving around the world. In my lifetime, I have seen many improvements in race relations, upward mobility of poor communities, and upgraded standards of living in communities around the globe. Qualities such as tranquility and compassion can be learned and taught to our children.

Eastern Origins of Meditation for Tranquility

Although all the studies mentioned above are recent, the importance of meditation for tranquility was established by the rishis (spiritual leaders of India) of the past, dating back to the era before Christ, who studied the human mind and its emotions. They developed several techniques to help us calm the mind and keep it in harmony with nature, the bounty God provided us when he created the universe. The rishis (also called yogis) mastered the practice of meditation and learned to control the body and the mind so that they are in harmony with the spirit, or the presence of God in us.

Meditation was popularized by Paramahansa Yogananda of Kolkata, India, who set up the Self-Realization Fellowship and its centers all over the United States. He first came to the U.S. in the 1930s and taught Kriya Yoga to his followers in California. Kriya Yoga is a simple psycho-physiological method by which inner turbulence can be calmed through meditation. We each have a choice as to what we want to do to achieve tranquility and remain tranquil. The scientific studies described in this essay explore the opportunities presented by daily meditation for tranquility in a healthy and productive life.

ESSAY 4

The Spiritual Basis of Tranquility

A religious man is a person who holds God and man in one thought at one time, at all times, who suffers harm done to others, whose greatest passion is compassion, whose greatest strength is love and defiance of despair.

— ABRAHAM JOSHUA HESCHEL

20th-century Jewish philosopher, theologian, and social activist

SPIRITUALITY MAY BE DEFINED as the quality of being concerned with the human soul or animating essence, as opposed to physical and material things. This sense of priority acknowledges that we are part of a greater whole which is transcendent or divine in nature. Swami Vivekananda, the great thinker from India who first visited the United States in 1893, said that "each soul is potentially divine."

Different peoples approach spirituality in different ways, and over time various approaches have emerged to form the world's religions. These religions preach that human beings are created in the image of God and may be tranquil by following their respective religious scriptures. There are three major Abrahamic religions: Judaism, Christianity, and Islam. One of the world's oldest religions, if not indeed *the* oldest,

87

is Hinduism, which has been practiced in the Indian subcontinent for over 10,000 years. Other smaller Eastern religions include Confucianism, practiced largely in China, and Buddhism, which has grown to have a worldwide following. Buddhism was one of many developments out of Hinduism at a time of great spiritual ferment. Gautama Buddha was originally a Hindu before he founded Buddhism to teach of seeking enlightenment and the path to Nirvana (eternal peace). Another smaller religion, this one coming out of Persia, is Zoroastrianism. This essay will describe the way three major religions—Hinduism, Islam, and Christianity—view and approach tranquility through their teachings.

All religions proclaim that there is one all-powerful God who created this universe and has laid out rules of conduct which will lead to a peaceful, tolerant society where humans can achieve their full potential and eventually reach God. Hinduism offers many gods to its followers to provide flexibility in their prayers, but in essence, there is only God who created this universe and prescribed the laws under which it will operate smoothly. By following the rules of conduct laid out in the religion, humans can coexist peacefully and lead happy, fulfilled lives. The laws prescribed by governments are further expansions of the rules of conduct provided in the religions so that society can function smoothly within a legal framework.

The Hindu Approach to Tranquility

In Hinduism, the Vedas are ancient texts that were given orally by God and transcribed by several rishis (or seers), who laid out detailed rules of conduct for performing various roles and rites in society and finally reaching Moksha (or complete release from the cycle of death and rebirth). The four pillars (or goals of human life) of Hinduism are

Dharma, Artha, Kama, and Moksha. Every Hindu is required to follow Dharma (or righteous conduct) in pursuit of Artha (security) and Kama (desires). Hindus believe everyone must continue to endure the cycle of reincarnation until they achieve sufficient self-knowledge to set them free through Moksha. The concept of reincarnation is a powerful incentive to do good and lead a tranquil life, as it promises either a better birth in the next life or freedom from the cycle of birth and death.

Dharma is the term signifying right living, the way in which humans are intended to pursue security and fulfillment of their desires. The Vedas describe the Dharma in detail, and they also prescribe many rituals that should be carried out in order to fulfill our desires and achieve a secure and happy life. The Hindu Dharma is the moral framework that, when it was followed correctly, enabled India to be prosperous for many millennia. However, this Dharma is not stressed enough in children's education today, and we thus see large inequities in Indian society. Corruption is on the increase because human greed has made many people forget the Dharmic values that have been passed down for over 10,000 years. Hence, the Vedas should be revived and the Dharmic values detailed in the Vedas should be emphasized as people pursue security and fulfillment of desires.

The pillar known as Artha refers to both financial and physical security. As we have mentioned elsewhere, there can be a fine line for some people between what is enough to live a good life and save for the future while contributing to society, and what seems never enough to fully secure one's future. Security is a mental attitude, and if the right attitude doesn't develop early in life according to dharmic values, it can lead to an ongoing sense of insecurity. The world has many problems, and we see crime in many parts of our cities and rural areas. We should do what we can to be safe, but we cannot focus excessively on things we cannot control.

I know some people who are never satisfied with what they have saved and are hesitant to part with their money to contribute to the needy in society. In his comprehensive book *Looking Away*,[20] author Harsh Mander notes how the middle and upper classes in Indian society have become uncaring for the needs of the poor people and are self-absorbed in their own lives. For them, family starts at home and ends with their children and grandchildren. The Bhagavad Gita tells us that anyone who takes all that society offers and does not give back in a like manner is a thief. Hence, the Gita tells us that charity, along with sacrifice and self-discipline, should be integral parts of everyone's life.

Physical and financial security finally come from being at peace with oneself and seeing the oneness of creation. When we observe the trees in nature, we see that they give unconditionally of their fruits and other benefits without demanding anything for themselves. If we care for them, they will survive and continue to give us clean air (since they take in carbon dioxide and give out oxygen), shade during hot days, and whatever else they have. Animals take only what they need to survive and leave the rest alone. Humans alone keep taking from nature and never seem to be satisfied with what they have. They always want more, even if others in society do not have their fair share. Hence, the Gita cautions us to limit our desires according to the Dharmic values laid out earlier, and to live a disciplined and peaceful life.

Kama, or desire, is the motivator for all our actions. When Kama is within the limits of Dharma, we achieve personal success and contribute

---

20 Harsh Mander, *Looking Away: Inequality, Prejudice and Indifference in New India* (Speaking Tiger, 2015).

to the welfare of society with innovations and our work. Self-discipline is the only way to limit our desires to our needs and not to indulge in wants that can be harmful to ourselves and also to the use of resources unsustainably. Kama is required for us to have children and bring up the next generation with the values that are important for a sustainable future.

Moksha, or salvation from this life to a better life in the future, is the fourth and ultimate pillar of the Hindu life. It refers to complete freedom or peace which is the ultimate goal of every human being. Buddhists call it Nirvana, or freedom from the sorrows inherent in life. Hindus believe in reincarnation, and Moksha allows them to break this cycle of birth and death and merge with God. When you analyze Artha and Kama carefully, they also strive for freedom and peace in this life. Most people realize the limits of Artha and Kama and come to Moksha eventually. The Vedas tell us that the best time to fulfill your Artha and Kama are in your working years, and that after retirement, one should focus on obtaining Moksha. Further, the Vedas tell us that our true nature is the soul within us, which is always free and peaceful. So realizing our true nature through spiritual practices during your retirement can lead to complete freedom and peace.

This is only possible if you develop a sense of detachment (called Vairagya) toward your possessions and family, and strive for inner peace and freedom. You come to realize that all sources of external happiness (from people and things) are temporary; they come and go. At that time, you focus on being happy within yourself. This portion of the Vedas that deal with spiritual practices that lead to self-realization is called Vedanta. The best-known proponent of Vedanta in the United States was Swami Vivekananda, who came to address the Parliament of Religions in Chicago in 1893. Vivekananda Vedanta

Societies are now present all over America and many parts of the world. They stress the universality of all religions and emphasize the importance of self-realization.

The Vedas have been divided into two main parts, with the first part called Karma Kanda, which prescribes duties and rituals for accomplishing all the desires you have in a Dharmic manner. It is very elaborate and has delineated rules for rituals to achieve every kind of happiness imaginable by a human being. The second part is called the Upanishads, which describe several ways of praying to God for getting you ready for Moksha. They also lay out in great detail the story of creation, describe how one is a potentially a divine soul, and provide the knowledge of and a road map to knowing yourself and becoming free of all worldly desires and wants.

In addition to the Vedas, the most important texts for Hindus are the Bhagavad Gita and the Brahma Sutras. These books give a comprehensive discussion of the source of our ignorance about our true nature and how one can remove this timeless ignorance with the light of knowledge about the permanent nature of our souls. The term used by Hindus for the soul is Atma. The Gita is a summary of the Vedas and is only 700 verses, and it has been my daily companion for the last 50 years.

The values described in essay 1 of this book, "Values-Based Living," are from the Bhagavad Gita. Those values—among which are respect for others, honesty, self-discipline, and forbearance—are conducive to tranquility, and the Gita gives a detailed guide to developing them in our competitive society. The two paths laid out in the Gita and the Vedas for destroying ignorance and gaining knowledge are Karma Yoga, or the path of action, and Jnana Yoga, or the path of knowledge, for the introspective person or intellectual. These paths form the basis for attaining and holding on to tranquility, even under the most stressful conditions we may face.

In Hindu teachings, universal consciousness is God and consists of the five elements: earth, water, air, fire, and space. These elements constitute the body and the entire universe. Earth sustains us through the food it provides, water and air are essential for life, fire keeps our body warm and provides the energy to cook our food, and space supports these four elements. The individual consciousness in every human being is a fraction of the universal consciousness, and the goal of life is to realize this universal consciousness that is in us and enlivens us. This is Moksha, or complete freedom. This realization, Moksha, calls for constant awareness and a sense of gratitude for all the things God has provided us.

Karma Yoga, the path of action that the Gita describes, is applicable to a majority of people and is the best way to avoid stress and live a tranquil life. Karma Yoga tells us that we should focus on the quality and content of our work, and that God will then decide what we deserve and give it to us. Once we come to accept the result He gives, we will be neither elated nor depressed with what we receive. With this acceptance comes tranquility, and we're ready to move on to our next task.

Karma Yoga also tells us that the effort we put into our work is only one of five factors that control the results of our work. The other four are the grace of God, the kind of environment we work in, the tools and/or skills we have to do our work, and the attitude we have toward our work. Of these five factors, we control only three: our effort, the skills we bring to the work, and our attitude. We do our best so that these three factors contribute as much as possible to our work, and we pray to God for the other two. Beyond this, we can make no claim to the results of our work, other than to accept whatever comes. This path, this Karma Yoga, relieves the anxiety and stress we face in our lives.

In a competitive world, it may feel like Karma Yoga is a utopian dream. If we analyze this statement, however, we may realize how shortsighted this view is. The more tranquil and stress-free we are, the more we can concentrate on the goal we have and reach it successfully. However, if, in the spirit of competition, we take shortcuts and try to get ahead of others by whatever means are at our disposal, we will always be afraid of getting caught and paying a huge price for this. The classic example of this is the investor Bernie Madoff, who died in disgrace in jail after amassing billions of dollars illegally. His own son revealed Madoff's misdeeds to the government, and he was sentenced to a lengthy jail term, during which he died. The lesson here, then, is that the best way to achieve your dream is to do your work diligently and accept whatever results. In the long run, you will achieve your dream while leading a tranquil life, in which you achieve work-life balance and become a contributor to society.

Karma Yoga was taught by the god Krishna to his disciple Arjuna in the midst of a battlefield. Arjuna was confused about killing his kith and kin during a righteous war to establish the rule of law in his land. But he was cleared of his doubts and decided to do his duty to preserve righteousness and to punish the wrongdoer. All of us can practice this eternal teaching that helps us confront the problems we face in life. The teaching is so simple that unless we analyze it carefully, we cannot understand its practicality in our day-to-day life. It simply states: "Do your duty well, and leave the results of your action to God's will. However, never consider inaction, since every human being is driven to action to survive."

As indicated earlier, the results of our actions are dependent on five factors, of which we have control over only three: our effort, our skill, and our attitude. So by not diverting our mind to anticipate the results of our action, we should do our best under the given circumstances and in the end, everything will turn out well. For doing this, we need to have faith in ourselves and in God. It is my personal experience that in the long run, everything turns out well if we keep doing what we have to do and don't stress ourselves about what might happen. I've reflected on situations in which I was stressed, and in hindsight, all the stress was unnecessary. Acceptance of "what is" is important, compared to "what could be."

The second part of the Vedas, the Upanishads, is also called Vedanta. This portion emphasizes the importance of knowing yourself, the consciousness that marks you as alive and is the eternal source of happiness. Our tendency is to focus on the body/mind as the essence of any human being, whereas Vedanta tells us that it is the inner consciousness or soul that is of paramount importance in helping you lead a peaceful and tranquil life. Vedanta also makes the point that the happiness that comes from interactions with things, people, or situations is temporary, that whatever comes and goes is essentially unreliable.

Instead, Vedanta concentrates on teaching humans to distinguish between temporary happiness and permanent happiness, and gives us a stepwise path to develop the 4 D's—dispassion, discrimination, discipline, and determination—to find the happiness within ourselves. Vedanta calls this source of happiness the Atma, or the God residing in your heart. This Atma is the prime mover that makes you alive, and if you pay attention to its presence within you, it will lead you to tranquility. Worldly pleasures are too attractive, and human weakness for these pleasures keeps us from the source of tranquility within us.

From childhood, our familiar sources of happiness are things that give us pleasure in the moment, such as something tasty to eat or a toy or friends. As we grow older, our toys become more sophisticated, we are choosy about selecting friends, and the range of things we prefer to eat, drink, and smoke increases exponentially. When we succumb to such sense pleasures, they can be gratifying in the short term but may become sources of pain or ill health in the long run. Objectively recognizing this aspect of sense pleasures is called Vairagya, or dispassion (detachment), in the Hindu religion. Unless one develops Vairagya, it is hard to practice the values-based life or the 9 Steps to Tranquility of this book's title.

Developing Vairagya requires inquiry into the sources of happiness in a process called Vichara. Unless you conduct this inquiry, you remain enmeshed in worldly pleasures and will keep going through alternating periods of happiness and sorrow. These are two sides of one coin, and just as you get heads or tails when you flip a coin, you will get happiness or sorrow depending entirely on factors beyond your control. Therefore, the Upanishads say, you must develop Vairagya, develop and strengthen the values-based life, and read the scriptures to find the source of tranquility that is within you—reading, reflection, and practice: Sravanam, Mananam, and Nidhidhyasana, in the Hindu tradition. Many years of performing these three disciplines will give you permanent happiness, and you will find the tranquility within yourself.

The Islamic Approach to Tranquility

The Quran, the holy book of Islam, offers a structured life for Muslims, filled with prayer, ritual, and a specific lifestyle. The five pillars of Islam are:

1. Profession of faith, called Shahada—the belief that there is no god but God, whom Muslims call Allah, and that Muhammad is the messenger of Allah, is the central theme of Islam
2. Prayer, or Salat—Muslims pray during five times every day and in a special weekly group prayer on Fridays
3. Alms, or Zakat
4. Fasting, or Sawm
5. Pilgrimage, called Hajj

These pillars are strictly followed by many traditional Muslims. The prayers help Muslims remain tranquil, and the other pillars help them live a disciplined life.

Irfan Hasan has written an excellent compilation of Islamic sayings in his book *Resilience, Positivity, Optimism, Inner Peace, Tranquility, Happiness, Eternal Bliss and Endless Triumph in an Age of Anxiety, Turbulence and Turmoil.*[21] His work summarizes the work of Imam Abu Hamid Muhammad Al-Ghazali (1058–1111 CE) and Maulana Jalaluddin Rumi (1207–1273 CE). He says that understanding the true purpose and worth of a human being allows one to eradicate all negativities within and transform one's life for the better. This transformation begins in the heart and soul of the human being, and as this inner light strengthens, it goes out and transforms entire communities, nations, and consequently, the world.

Hasan delineates four aspects of eternal happiness and endless success central to Islam:

---

21 Irfan Hasan, *Resilience, Positivity, Optimism, Inner Peace, Tranquility, Happiness, Eternal Bliss and Endless Triumph in an Age of Anxiety, Turbulence and Turmoil* (Independently Published, 2021).

1.   Knowing one's own self
2.   Knowing God
3.   Knowing the reality of the world
4.   Knowing the reality of the hereafter

Hasan says that knowing the above four things is, in fact, the essence of Islam. Two of those types of knowledge relate to the inner self, and two relate to the outer self. The essential elements of the outer self are:

1.   To obey the commands of God (called Dharma in Hinduism)
2.   To keep them in view in the matter of one's dealings with the world

The essential elements of the inner self are:

1.   To keep the heart (soul) purified from all bad morals, such as anger, miserliness, arrogance, pride, etc.
2.   To adorn the heart (soul) with good morals, such as patience, gratitude, love, hope, trust in God, etc.

Just as Hinduism says that God is your inner self and that if you dwell within that inner self (happy with yourself), you will realize God, Islam says that in recognizing your inner self, you know God. There-fore, in Islam, the essence of a tranquil life is to be inward-focused, instead of outward-focused to the pleasures of the worldly life. As we realize during our journey through life, there is no end to the pleasures of the world and those pleasures are fleeting. As soon as one pleasur-able experience is over, the mind craves the next one, which it wants to be better than the previous experience. All religions proclaim that the true source of lasting happiness is within yourself, and you can find it in solitude. That is the reason many religions suggest a regular retreat from the pressures of the worldly life.

In Islam, according to Hasan, one has no alternative but to say that God knows best. He notes the following four characteristics of God (or Allah):

1. God is omnipotent.
2. God is omnipresent.
3. He is responsible for the continuous motion of the stars and constellations.
4. He grants sustenance for all living creatures.

Much of Hasan's book is devoted to discussing what leads to failure in spirituality, and thus drowns us in constantly seeking happiness outside of ourselves. He describes desire and anger (termed Raaga and Dwesha in Hinduism) as two servants of the heart, and if they become subservient to the soul and obey the inner voice, he says, a person can be spiritually successful and gain lasting happiness. Hasan likens the human intellect to a wise person that can repel the deception and fraud of Satan (the never-ending sensual pleasures) and use the intellect's deep insight and reason to annihilate the temptations of the world (lust and anger). He advises us to keep a watchful eye on our movements and stillness, speech and silence, and to listen to the voice of conscience. Otherwise, we can sink into the foul conditions of shamelessness, vileness, wastefulness, ostentation, defamation, immorality, greed, lust, jealousy, enmity, and other vices.

The primary benefit of saying that God knows best is that you don't second-guess yourself and you therefore avoid many regrets. You will do your best in any field of action and leave the result to God, since he knows best what you deserve. (This Islamic precept has a parallel in Hinduism in Karma Yoga.) Hasan quotes from the Quran, chapter 13, verse 28, which says, "Verily, hearts find peace and tranquility in the remembrance of God." He says further, "A believer's heart is clean (and illumined and enlightened) with a lamp lit up in it (that exudes light through its clarity and brilliance on account of one's spiritual strivings for its transformation towards everything positive). A non-believer's heart is dark and turned upside down." (In Hinduism, this is called Shraddha, or faith.)

Hasan describes four types of hearts from Islamic teachings:

1. One heart is clean and has a lamp lit in it; that is the heart of the believer.
2. One type of heart is dark and upside down; that is the heart of the non-believer.
3. One type of heart is enveloped in a covering and its opening is closed; that is the heart of the hypocrite.
4. One type of heart has both faith and hypocrisy coexisting in it.

Hasan also talks about two ways of acquiring knowledge. One method is through the five senses, by means of which the knowledge comes through the observation and study of various subjects. The other method is to close those sensory channels of knowledge acquisition and to go deeper to such an extent that the fountains of knowledge start to emanate from within. This can happen only when the heart is meticulously purified and cleansed, and the veils are lifted from it (to unveil the spiritual realities).

The message conveyed by Hasan in the previous paragraphs is similar to that in verse 6 of chapter 6 of the Bhagavad Gita, which essentially says: For one who has conquered his lower Self (anger and desire) by exercising the higher Self (knowledge and justice), his Self is a friend; but for he who has not conquered his lower Self, his Self is an enemy. So, as we examine each major religion, it seems to be emerging clearly that spirituality in every tradition urges us to conquer our lower impulses, such as anger and desire, and to strive to attain tranquility by using the higher powers of knowledge and justice (the inner voice of our consciousness).

Hasan has dedicated a chapter of his book to how attachment to worldly life, possessions, and power, and then making these the purpose of one's life, leads one to commit moral errors and to the loss of tranquility. We have seen that repeatedly in Wall Street and the financial industry when some people attach such a high value to money that they break laws and end up in jail. Bernie Madoff, mentioned earlier, is a classic example. Hasan observes that detachment from worldly life helps put everything in correct perspective, freeing one's body, mind, intellect, and soul from being devoured by meaningless endeavors that consume the biggest capital one has: the limited time of one's life. Using this time well fosters inner peace, tranquility, peace with oneself, and peace with all fellow human beings.

According to a Sufi sage that Hasan quotes, "When I think of world and worldly life as great, I feel I am a mere atom in the cosmos, but when I think of worldly life as small, then I find that the world is an atom and I am the master of this cosmos." So unless you put everything in correct perspective and learn to balance your worldly life with the time required to discover your inner peace, you will not have tranquility.

Hasan details a list from the Quran of eight benefits of leading a spiritual life:

1. If you make your good deeds your beloved, they will go with you to your grave, and will become an illuminated candle in your grave and will never separate from you.
2. You conquer your lower desires and find peace in the worship of God, the Exalted.
3. You live a life of charity and giving, and these are deposited with God and you live a good life here and hereafter.
4. You are never proud of your family and wealth, but use it for the welfare of others, and thus are ranked highest in the sight of God.
5. You have no jealousy of anyone and get along with everyone in the world.
6. You live a life of discipline and follow the commandments of God and worship Him.
7. You do the right thing to earn a livelihood, with the firm belief that God will bring the sustenance He has promised in the Quran.
8. You place your trust in God instead of on wealth or people around you.

He says that "whoever acts on these eight principles is like as if one has acted on all four holy books of the Torah, Quran, Bible and Zabur (psalms)."

Hasan concludes by saying that "each one of us can choose to deal with them [the variegated situations we find ourselves in] positively by drawing deeper into the reservoirs of one's own inner spiritual resources, buried deep with the innermost recesses of our soul, and using them and one's own unique situation and challenges to completely transform oneself for the better." This inner transformation unleashes our true potential that, in turn, brings about a positive transformation around us at various levels. Hasan notes that it is never too late to embark upon your own self-realization to attain the real purpose of life and consequent eternal happiness and everlasting triumph. The first step needed from you is your desire to change for the better, and for that purpose, you will need to bring an open heart and mind to explore the previously unchartered waters.

What I find most striking is the similarity between the Islamic and Hindu approaches to tranquility. Both talk of achieving self-realization by looking within ourselves and of not seeking tranquility through the outside world, with which we deal daily for our work and in maintaining our relations with others. Sadly, however, dogmatic leaders and their followers in both religions choose to spread hate and speak ill of the other religion. They seek to divide people based on their respective religions, instead of seeing the universality of spirit that permeates us all.

I was taught in a Christian school in India until high school, and I realized at a young age that what my Christian teachers were telling me was essentially the same as what I was learning at home from my parents, who practiced Hinduism. The main thing I learned in school was to "treat my neighbor as I would like to be treated," and I was never told that you do this only if your neighbor is the same religion as yourself.

It is my firm belief that this universality of all religions and their spiritual teaching should be taught in all schools around the world to foster world peace, starting with the tranquility in ourselves. This could lead to tolerance among all religions and cultures, and allow us to become richer as a species on this planet.

The Christian Approach to Tranquility

Christianity is practiced by over a billion people in the world. The Ten Commandments, originally given in the Jewish faith, are also accepted as part of Christianity. Although there are many denominations within the Christian faith, this section of the essay will focus on the Catholic Church and its teachings.

Catholics believe that Jesus Christ, the son of God, came to earth to save human beings from sin and lead them to salvation. Sin can be considered any thought, word, or action that is in opposition to the Ten Commandments and the teachings of Jesus. In John Stott's book *Basic Christianity*,[22] he mentions the consequences of sin as being of three types:

1. Upon God
2. Upon ourselves
3. Upon our fellow humans

A person's highest destiny is to know God and to be in a personal relationship with Him. Sin cuts us off from God and His teachings. Stott says that many people feel abandoned when they do not have a personal relationship with God. He says, "We feel burdened by our sins and this accounts for the restlessness of men and women today. There

---

22 John Stott, *Basic Christianity* (InterVarsity Press, 2021).

is a hunger in the heart which none can satisfy, a vacuum which only God can fill." When we are restless, it negatively impacts our relationship with others and our own tranquility. Stott says it is important to obey the First Commandment, which concerns our duty to God. We are to love our God first, and then our neighbor as ourselves.

So God's order is that we put Him first, others next, and ourselves last. Sin is the reversal of this order. Sin not only estranges; it enslaves. Sin is an inward corruption of human nature, and we are in bondage. It is not so much certain acts or habits which enslave us but rather the evil source from which these spring. If we want to live a tranquil life, we have to free ourselves from this bondage of self-centeredness. Bishop Robert Barron, a well-known author and proponent of the Christian faith, says that there are seven deadly sins, and of these, the worst is pride. The others are:

- Envy
- Anger
- Sloth
- Avarice
- Gluttony
- Lust

With God's help and guidance, we can overcome these sins and live a tranquil life.

In his book *To Light a Fire on the Earth: Proclaiming the Gospel in a Secular Age*,[23] Robert Barron identifies God as the creator, from whom all of creation came forth. The five arguments are:

---

23 Robert Barron, with John L. Allen, *To Light a Fire on the Earth: Proclaiming the Gospel in a Secular Age* (Image Books, 2017).

1. He is the unmoved mover, who makes all the changes that we see in the world.
2. He is the first cause, because something has to exist without being caused, and that is God.
3. He is the One who is not contingent on anything, who got the ball rolling.
4. He is the absolute standard of perfect goodness, perfect beauty, and so on, against which everything else is judged.
5. He is the intelligent force that gave us the Laws on which the universe operates.

Barron urges us all to become one with God, not the servant of God. (This is the exact message that the Hindu scriptures give to all believers, and it is called Moksha, the ultimate freedom in this universe.) His advice to all humans is to find God's gift in us and dedicate our lives to God by helping others in need.

In addressing the relation between science and God, Barron says that "the sciences can shed light on a whole range of questions that human beings find intensely interesting, but what is beautiful? What makes something morally right or wrong? What is the nature of reality? What does it mean to be true? What is the nature of consciousness? These questions are not reducible to the sciences."

Barron says that truth, beauty, and goodness are the key elements of Christianity. His words of advice to all believers in God is that Jesus's way of nonviolence and love, a path not of this world but that appears in our world, is the only way to overcome the dysfunctions in our life that sin brings. The inspirational people who make an appearance in essay 6 are those who have exhibited the qualities of nonviolence and love, and these people have inspired millions of people to find meaning in their lives and live a life of complete freedom. Jesus inspired the gospels, his messengers, and many saints in the world to spread the message of love and nonviolence and to make the world a better place.

In his book *Tranquility: Cultivating a Quiet Soul in a Busy World*,[24] David W. Henderson talks about the many ways of nurturing serenity in the midst of our busy world. He also speaks about Soul Satisfaction and mentions five questions most people ask. These are:

1. Who am I? (what defines me)
2. What is the reason for my being? (having purpose in life)
3. Is what I do important? (the uniqueness and significance of what I do)
4. Am I worthwhile? (my intrinsic worth, irrespective of what I do)
5. Am I loved? (being valued and accepted for I you am)

God, our creator, says Henderson, answers these questions in the following ways:

1. I created you uniquely and you belong to Me.
2. To live for Me and to love those I place around you. (The central teaching in the Hindu scriptures is that you offer all your work as a worship to God, and accept what He gives, since this gives you immediate mental tranquility.)
3. Yes, everyone has a unique duty to make society function well.

---

24 David W. Henderson, *Tranquility: Cultivating a Quiet Soul in a Busy World* (Baker Books, 2015).

4. Yes, you are valuable since there is no one like you.

5. Yes, you are in My image and I am present in you.

Once we understand the basic answers God has given here (taken from many Biblical passages), we can live a productive and tranquil life. The reason most people don't understand these answers, says Henderson, is that they are caught in the busyness trap, which he defines as "trying to fit an infinite number of activities into a finite amount of time." This trap fuels our stress and robs our peace, raises our blood pressure and lowers our effectiveness. The tranquility solution to this busyness trap is to not try to do it all but rather to discern what God wants us to do, in the way and at the time that God wants us to do it, and to trust Him with the rest.

My own experience bears out the value of Henderson's tranquility solution. I have had a successful career running my own business, both in the United States and India, and participating in many charitable activities involving my time, talent, and money, also in the United States and India. And I was able to do this only because I have followed the tranquility solution described by Henderson. I discerned that God wants me to do the following:

1. Do my religious duties (prayers and time with God) every morning (irrespective of whatever else is happening in my life), have a healthy breakfast, and be punctual to work

2. Focus on my work, satisfy my clients, and work well with the team to accomplish my daily goals

3. Come home on time to have dinner with my family, and spend time with them

4. Do my evening prayers, and sleep at the same time every night so I am rested up for another day

Henderson brings up an important caution given by Jesus in Matthew 6:34: "Do not worry about tomorrow, for tomorrow will worry about itself. Each day has trouble enough of its own." By remembering this simple caution, and by not regretting the past, about which you can do nothing (except learn from it), you can live a tranquil life. You can make the most out of the present time, a gift from God, and do your best every day.

Henderson describes the soil in which the fruit of the Spirit is grown, listing the following characteristics of the person in which the Spirit grows, which also help us remain tranquil:

- Love
- Joy
- Peace
- Patience
- Kindness
- Goodness
- Faithfulness
- Self-control

By absorbing these characteristics, Henderson explains, you can learn to find joy in God rather than in circumstances, to be at peace with matters outside of your control, to be patient with annoyances, to be kind to the weak and struggling, to pursue goodness rather than ambition, to let God grow large as you recede into a spirit of gentle humility, … and to let God, rather than feelings, control you.

Henderson talks of three rhythms in our life, the first being the daily cycle of wakefulness and sleep, the second the weekly pattern of work and rest, and the third, most important one being the routine cycle of engagement and disengagement, of forward motion followed by retreat into solitude and silence. Achieving stillness is a prerequisite to encountering God. "Be still" must come before "and know that I am God" (Psalm 46:10). Along with stillness, silence is crucial to the health of the soul. Henderson quotes Mark 6:31, where Jesus urged his followers, "Come with Me by yourself to a quiet place and get some rest." He suggests spending time in nature as often as possible to find the stillness and peace in ourselves. This has proved true in the morning walks I enjoy taking in the nearby forest preserve, just listening to the birds and watching an occasional deer cross my path. I get exercise, feel healthy, and am rested in spirit so as to sustain my regular routine.

Henderson concludes with the statement that "Tranquility comes on the other side of relinquishment, not accomplishment." I have found this to be the case throughout my busy career of 44 years. Whenever I become anxious about the result of any project I've undertaken, I become stressed and make questionable decisions. I was doing a new project in India with a partner of mine, and he promised me things were going well. Suddenly he called me one day and said we can do this project only if you send me another $5,000. I was so stressed about the project's success that I didn't even pause to think why things weren't going well, why he was suddenly asking me for extra money, or what the prospects of success for the project were. After I had sent the money, and other people involved has invested more money, too, I found out that my partner was misusing the funds and the project was failing. I learned a valuable lesson: that I should not get so fixed on a project's results but focus rather on doing what is rational and on yielding the result to God. If I had behaved as I should have, tranquility would have reigned throughout the process.

Summary

It appears from what we've seen of all three of the religions we've examined—Hinduism, Islam, and Christianity—that the most important requirement for leading a tranquil life is to follow the teachings of God and do your best for yourself, your family, and your community. The importance of being thoughtful about what we desire is the crux of all religions, and each religion stresses the value of charity, of sharing our resources with those who are not as fortunate as we are. Hinduism stresses that charity, sacrifice, and discipline are the duties of every Hindu and should never be given up. Jesus Christ told his disciples to live a simple life and always love others as they wished to be loved. The five pillars of Islam also stress the importance of a disciplined life and of offering charity to those in society who need help.

Health, both physical and mental, and happiness of the deep and enduring kind both spring from the disciplined living promoted in a values-based life and in all the religious scriptures. These help us maintain a clear conscience, which in turn leads to tranquility. The key aids to tranquility talked about in these three religions include:

1. Having a regular routine, with time devoted to scriptures and prayers, work, family, and personal well-being. This personal custom or schedule can help you avoid sin and lead a good life.

2. Doing your best every day and leaving the result of your work in God's hands. Because you can't control all aspects that influence the result you want, it's best to understand that you get what you deserve and to accept it gracefully.

3. Devoting a portion of your time, treasure, and talent to help the needy in your community. Every religion varies, but most suggest at least 5–10 percent of your income should be dedicated to charity.

4. Treat everyone with love, respect, and compassion, and you will receive the same from most others in return.

5. Keep the company of good people, and you will make progress toward more tranquility in your life.

ESSAY 5

Why Is Tranquility Important?

We humans have lost the wisdom of genuinely resting and relaxing.
We worry too much. We don't allow our bodies to heal, and we don't
allow our minds and hearts to heal.

—THICH NHAT HANH

Vietnamese Buddhist monk, teacher, and peace activist

IMAGINE YOU ARE FACING a big report deadline for an important client. Suddenly, your computer crashes and your work file is lost. Irretrievably lost, it seems. What's more, you have a child who is not well and needs your attention. Under such circumstances, stress builds up, leaving you at a loss as to how to handle the various responsibilities. You can't think straight and you spend a sleepless night worrying about everything.

How do you handle this stress? If these kinds of stressful situations happen a lot, they will definitely impact your health and happiness. It's precisely at moments like these, however, that a knowledge and practice of tranquility can not only save your day but make an ongoing difference in your professional and personal lives. With a tranquil mind, you can sort out your priorities. You can call your client, explain the situation, and get a few more days to finish the work. You can take care of your child, have the computer fixed, retrieve the lost material with specialized software, and finish your report for the client.

Managing situations like this makes tranquility important in your life. Other sorts of reasons to cultivate a tranquil mind include:

- Managing life's ups and downs
- Staying healthy, physically and emotionally
- Managing stressful situations calmly
- Achieving professional and financial success

Making alert living an integral part of your life offers many benefits—good health, peace of mind, professional and personal success. And to change your life dramatically and enjoy the benefits of a tranquil life, you need to first analyze your situation fully and decide to make the effort to prepare your mind for incorporating the steps proposed in this book.

Managing Life's Ups and Downs

Once you've lived a few years as an adult, you begin to realize the truth in the maxim that the only constant in life is change. Pleasurable experiences can be replaced by unpleasant ones with little or no notice. So unless you're prepared to adjust to the ups and downs, you won't find life easy to navigate, if you can manage to at all. What's more, when reactions to things beyond your control make your life fluctuate constantly from happy to unhappy, you become unreliable to others.

The Bhagavad Gita, a celebrated part of Mahabharata, one of the major Hindu scriptures, written some 2,000 years ago, refers to the paired human emotions Raaga and Dwesha, meaning, respectively, intense desire for some things/people and intense hatred of some things/people. The message of the Gita is that unless you learn how to handle these opposing emotions in a balanced manner, your life will be out of your control. Similarly, you have to learn well to balance the ups and downs of your life to gain tranquility.

In my teens, I went through a series of ups and downs, and learned how to handle them by absorbing the teachings of the Gita. When I graduated from high school, I was confident I would have the grades required for me to enter engineering college. I studied very hard, but when I didn't get the grades I wanted, I became dejected. My elder brother counseled me that I was just starting life and if I didn't learn to manage these unexpected turns, I'd find it nearly impossible to succeed and achieve my dream of becoming an engineer. I listened to him and continued my studies, also participating in extracurricular activities such as the Reserve Officers Training Corps (called National Cadet Corps [NCC] in India). I excelled in college and achieved the highest rank in the NCC. After two years of pursuing my bachelor's degree in science, I applied to the local engineering college, and due to my high rank in the NCC, I was selected for the course in mining engineering. That transformed my life, and I retired in 2018 after a 44-year career in engineering.

This lesson learned at a young age helped me develop a balanced attitude toward the ups and downs life has dealt me, and to extend that lesson about tranquility throughout my life. When you analyze facts and deal with them objectively, you can respond to any situation with composure instead of being overwhelmed emotionally.

In dealing with the ultimate sorrow, the death of a loved one, the Bhagavad Gita counsels that death is natural for anyone who is born and should be accepted with grace. The law of karma, described in detail in the Gita, says that a person's behavior and values are based on what they did in their previous lives, and that a person reaps what they sow. With your free will and efforts to improve in the current life, you can change your life for the better.

The law of karma gives Hindu believers some solace about deaths we cannot explain, of young people of dying of cancer or some rare disease, or of loss of life in a horrible accident. Religious faith is another important guide in managing happiness and sorrow in a balanced manner and not wasting life in deep sorrow or depression. The message in all scriptures, in fact, is to have faith in God to manage the things we cannot control, and that we do our best every day to improve ourselves.

Staying Healthy, Physically and Emotionally

It seems almost too obvious to say that physical and emotional health are of great importance to anyone who would be successful in life and reach their goals. However, it's less widely understood that tranquility can place the state of your health largely under your own control, rather than leaving it to be dictated by outside circumstances. People and situations beyond your control are always changing, and not always in ways that are in your favor. But with a tranquil mind, you can accept these changes without blaming others or complaining of the world being against you.

Controlling your emotions while reacting to life's daily changes is an important part of staying healthy and productive. Before reacting to a situation, try to ask yourself the following questions:

- Do I have to react, or can I let it go?

- Is what I am going to say helpful to the situation, or will it aggravate it?
- How can I express my reaction without being defensive or getting angry?
- Will it hurt me and the other person if I react to the situation? Sometimes we simply react without thinking of the consequences to ourselves and others. So being alert and reacting only when necessary is one instance of tranquil living.

The connection between body and mind, and their influence on one another, has been well established by science and medicine over the years. There are a number of recorded instances of people whose mental mastery has allowed them to live long and healthy lives. This mental mastery was critical in order for Mahatma Gandhi to lead India to independence while suffering insults and physical and emotional pain during British rule. His patient self-control over a period of some 27 years allowed him to win over the hearts of British and Indian alike, finally realizing his goal. When you learn to bring your mind under your control, it can serve you instead of bringing you harm through rampant emotions. This is especially important in managing your personal and professional relations.

Building a disciplined life with control of your sense organs is challenging, but it can be accomplished with regular practice. We have five senses, experienced through the eyes (vision), ears (hearing), nose (smell), tongue (taste), and skin (touch). The senses bring us knowledge of the outside world and help us enjoy life. If we learn to discipline, for example, our eyes by reducing their exposure to violent movies, our mind can remain calm. It is easy to binge-watch streaming videos for hours, but this kind of activity—or inactivity—will inevitably impact our health by getting in the way of truly restful sleep. Listening to loud music for many years will adversely affect our hearing and lead to other health issues. If we overindulge in fatty foods or other unhealthy foods merely to satisfy our cravings, we will pay dearly with weight gain and very possibly related conditions that can limit enjoyment of life. In our modern culture of instant gratification, the control of our senses—that is, making them part of our overall aim to lead a disciplined and purposeful life—is a real challenge. But for the sake of your own health and well-being, it is a challenge worth taking up.

The Bhagavad Gita says that whatever is like poison in the beginning, and in the end is sweet like nectar, is the source of true happiness. This can be understood to mean that with early years of practice, a disciplined, self-controlled life, which is very hard to achieve in the beginning, is well worth the initial sacrifice of material happiness because of the good health and tranquility ultimately experienced. The Gita calls this disciplined, tranquil lifestyle Sattvic Living and urges every human being to strive for this kind of life. In contrast, Rajasic Living finds a person indulging in sensual pleasures and paying for the indulgence with poor health and long-term physical and emotional problems. In Tamasic Living, the worst kind of life, according to the Gita, laziness and inactivity predominate and life loses any meaning. A person instead merely drags from day to day, shouldering mountains of problems.

These Hindu teachings are but one instance among many in the world of how a disciplined and tranquil life is key to physical and emotional health. Such a life, and the health benefits that attend it, help make possible your other goals, in business and in your community and your personal relationships.

Managing Stressful Situations Calmly

The hypothetical situation described at this essay's beginning happens daily throughout the world. We're all connected to our cell phones and laptops, and carry our work in our heads during the week and sometimes on weekends. We have other responsibilities as well, but we nonetheless need personal time to reinvigorate and become fully productive again.

Managing stress is an art that we must learn and includes learning how to clearly line up our priorities. Many of us have determined that work is our first priority—or at least we behave that way—and our family and personal life and our health all suffer.

During my 44-year professional career, I employed these priorities:

1. Health, both physical and emotional
2. Family, including my wife, child, and parents
3. Work

Under these priorities, which I made clear to my clients and fellow workers, I lived a largely stress-free life throughout most of my career. I worked efficiently, completing tasks during office hours and rarely bringing projects home to handle. I mentored young colleagues and delegated some work so I could focus on the most important tasks for my clients. These efficiencies meant I could spend quality time with my wife and child, and enjoy vacations at least twice a year. I also took time to visit my parents (who lived in India) and, when possible, had them visit me.

Another area of stress in our lives comes from the agendas and prejudices that we cultivate in our mind. These mental constructs reduce our capacity to think objectively and clearly. To counter this human tendency and the stress it creates, Swami Dayanand Saraswati, a great Hindu teacher, established Teaching Centers in the U.S. and India, and taught a process that he called developing an Objective Viewpoint.

With the aid of this Viewpoint, your subjectivity (including your agenda and prejudices) does not influence your assessment of a situation or a person. You realize that many situations cannot be changed, and that you cannot change anyone, but that you *can* change how you think and act.

You objectively assess the facts and the situation you are dealing with, and then take the best action you can—leaving the result in God's hands. This attitude of acceptance can dramatically minimize the stress you feel and can help you learn from all experiences. Ultimately, it can help you realize that there are no failures in life.

Achieving Professional and Financial Success

Susan, a young professional woman, works very hard to be the best in her field. But she finds it hard in a competitive world to find the right opportunities to showcase her talents. She has become highly frustrated after several years of professional experience, and she feels stress daily. She's sacrificed her other interests to do well in her career, but she still doesn't feel a sense of accomplishment. In the end, she doesn't feel motivated and hasn't found a purpose to her life.

Unfortunately, many professionals seem to find themselves in this situation. For Susan to find purpose and feel fulfilled, she will doubtless need to modify her attitude and, indeed, her approach to life. She needs a more tranquil life, one that allows her to balance her career and other interests, while paying attention to her health and family needs. With those changes, she should be able to achieve the professional and financial satisfaction she has sought.

Success isn't accurately measured by comparing yourself with your peers but by comparing where and how you started out with the change you've been able to achieve through your own efforts. You can't know everything your peers go through, either positive or negative, or what fate has in store for them. What you *can* know is that you've done your best every day. And you can accept what life has to offer you. This outlook help you create a tranquil mind, which in turn helps you address the challenges you'll face in life.

One measure of financial success lies in how independent you are from reliance on others. The old saying "Cut your coat according to your cloth" reflects another aspect, that is, limit what you do to in light of the resources you have. If you are able to meet your own needs, live within your means, and save even a bit for the future, you are a financial success.

Tranquility can provide you with the frame of mind to help you realize personal success and live a life that's happy and contented. That success—a deep and meaningful success—derives from learning to stay at ease with what you have and doing your best under the circumstances you meet with. In a way, there is no actual limit to one's needs; some people's "needs" expand with the amount of money they have to spend. Many of us know or know of professionals who live far beyond their means; and when things go wrong in the workplace or the economy, as we have seen during the recent pandemic, they are highly stressed and despondent.

We have seen innumerable Americans who never stood in line for food donations line up during these hard times to feed their families. If our tranquil mindset guides us to plan for such contingencies—which we now realize can happen at any time—we are able to weather any storm. I came to the U.S. to pursue higher studies. With hard work and a tranquil mind, I was able to achieve professional and financial success that I had never dreamed of . . . perhaps because I didn't spend much time dreaming of it. You have to act on your dreams, and with consistent effort and some luck, you can achieve what you aim for in life.

ESSAY 6

Leadership & Tranquility: Six Inspirational Stories

*Peace is not a relationship of nations. It is a condition of mind
brought about by a serenity of soul.*

— JAWAHARLAL NEHRU

author and statesman, the first prime minister of independent India

THE FOLLOWING PAGES CONTAIN brief sketches of some remarkable people, all of them world leaders who remained tranquil under demanding circumstances and achieved great things for the people who looked to them for direction. Although these leaders have worked in different fields—politics, finance, science, and humanitarian work—they share a spiritual approach to life and have exhibited the values discussed throughout this book.

These individuals have demonstrated for all of us, each on a very public stage, what human beings can accomplish when they stay focused on their goals while remaining tranquil in the face of ever-changing hardships and challenges. They faced great opposition in society to their ideas about helping people, but they worked on because they believed in the value of every human being.

Each life noted here has, in his or her own way, guided my own, and I hope their stories will inspire you to continue to seek for tranquility under all circumstances and achieve meaning throughout your life.[25] These leaders' names are:

- Mohandas Karamchand Gandhi
- Nelson Mandela
- Barack Obama
- Mother Teresa
- Warren Buffet
- A. P. J. Abdul Kalam

Mohandas Karamchand Gandhi

Mohandas Karamchand Gandhi was a clear choice for me because of the tranquility he brought to bear under the extremely difficult circumstances he faced during the independence struggle for a free India. He was born in 1869 in the city of Porbandar, in Gujarat state, India. By the time of his death in 1948, he had been given the loving title of Mahatma, which means "exalted soul," by the people of India, whom he had served tirelessly since returning to India after doing some groundbreaking work in South Africa against apartheid.

Gandhi was assassinated on January 30, 1948, by a Hindu extremist, Nathuram Godse, for his work toward peace between Hindus and Muslims. The British left India in August 1947, and their last act was to

---

25 I have used Wikipedia (www.en.wikipedia.org) and Biography (www.biography.com) as sources for some facts about my subjects' lives but have written their stories based on how they have impacted my life. I have analyzed their accomplishments and seen the effect and value of tranquility in their lives. I hope the reader will take note of and imbibe the same.

partition the country into two countries, Hindu India and Muslim Pakistan. Basing the partition on the religious beliefs of two large segments of Indian society resulted in the deaths of millions who tried, based on their religion, to leave one country and go to the other. Gandhi was deeply disturbed by the magnitude of the death and destruction created by the partition, and he worked intently to ensure peace among Muslims and Hindus in the new India.

Mahatma Gandhi was always my ideal from a young age, since my parents named me after a famous prayer of the Mahatma. Gandhi was assassinated on January 30, 1948, and I was born a week later. Hence, my parents named me Rajaram, a name of the Hindu god that was frequently used by Gandhi at his prayer meetings every evening during the independence struggle. As I heard about his life story from my parents while growing up, I was fascinated as to how a human being could sacrifice everything and live such a simple life (wearing only a loin cloth and a sheet covering his body) to understand the plight of the poor in colonial India. He gave up his family life to lead his country to freedom from Great Britain, the most powerful country in the world in the 20th century. His struggle for freedom started when he faced discrimination while serving as a lawyer in South Africa. His book *The Story of My Experiments with Truth*[26] covers his life from early childhood to the year 1921. I was fascinated by his frankness in the book, and it turned my life around as I analyzed my own life and tried my best to emulate his life of being true to himself and serving the larger society.

Gandhi's life in apartheid South Africa was a turning point for him. (Apartheid was a formally recognized social policy that sanctioned racial

---

26 Mohandas Karamchand Gandhi, *The Story of My Experiments with Truth* (Navajivan Press, 1927).

segregation and discrimination against nonwhites.) He had gone to South Africa to practice law and help the Indians who had settled there with their legal issues. He was shocked by the local laws that discriminated against the Hindus and the Indians generally. In 1906 he organized his first mass civil-disobedience campaign, which he called Satyagraha, meaning "truth and firmness." In the face of his relentless campaign (during which he was arrested and sent to jail), the government negotiated an agreement with Gandhi, which included the abolition of the poll tax for Indians and recognition of Hindu marriages. This success in South Africa helped him become a leader back home in India's freedom struggle from British rule.

Upon returning to India in January 1915, Gandhi founded an ashram (spiritual community) in Ahmedabad, Gujarat, India. This ashram, called the Sabarmati ashram, was open to all castes, and he fought the scourge of untouchability in India from this ashram. He devoted his life to prayer, fasting, and meditation and started preparing his own clothes (a loin cloth and shawl) using a spinning wheel. This became the symbol of freedom for India, and it is seen in the middle of the Indian flag. The Indian government has made the first week of January one to celebrate the contribution of Indians abroad to India's progress and development.

Gandhi opposed the occupation of India by the British. After he settled down at the Sabarmati Ashram in Gujarat, he made connections with people in the Indian National Congress. After he joined the Indian National Congress, there was an incident that shocked him in the neglected garden area of Jallianwala Bagh, in Amritsar, the Punjab, in April 1919. The British government had passed the Rowlatt Act to extend the emergency powers that they had promulgated during World War I. In opposition to this act, peaceful demonstrators had gathered in

Jallianwala Bagh. General Dyer of the British government ordered his troops to shoot the demonstrators. Some 400 people were killed and many more wounded. This sparked outrage throughout the country, and Gandhi led peaceful protests against the British for this inhumane action.

Mahatma Gandhi became a leading figure in the Indian Home Rule movement started by the Indian National Congress. He mobilized the citizens to stop serving the British government that was keeping India subservient and ruining the education system that had been working well for thousands of years. He urged them to stop paying taxes and purchasing goods imported from Britain. In order to encourage people to produce their own clothing, he began to use a portable spinning wheel to produce his own cloth. This cloth became popularly known as khadi, and all officials of Congress wore only clothes made of khadi instead of imported British fabric.

The spinning wheel became a symbol of Indian independence and self-reliance, called Swaraj. The Swaraj movement spread fast into the villages of India, where it was called Gram Swaraj. I was influenced by the Gram Swaraj movement and, with a few friends, and started an organization in Chicago named the India Development Coalition of America. Our organization worked toward mobilizing U.S. nonprofits to work for the sustainable development of rural India.

Gandhi fought for Hindu-Muslim unity in India throughout his life. In the end, he paid for his activism, since he was assassinated by a Hindu fundamentalist who felt Gandhi was favoring Muslims over Hindus after the partition of India. He began a three-week fast in the autumn of 1924 to urge unity between the two religions, and he focused on this cause until 1930. In that year, he returned to politics and protested against Britain's Salt Acts, which not only prohibited Indians from collecting or selling salt (a dietary staple) but imposed a heavy tax that hit the country's poorest particularly hard. Gandhi planned a new civil disobedience Satyagraha campaign, which is famously known as the Dandi Salt March.

The Dandi Salt March was a remarkable event in which ordinary citizens walked for 390 kilometers to the Arabian Sea. Before starting the march, Gandhi wrote to the British viceroy, Lord Irwin, that "my ambition is no less than to convert the British people through non-violence and thus make them see the wrong they have done in India." Wearing a homespun white shawl and sandals and carrying a walking stick, Gandhi walked to the coastal town of Dandi on the Arabian Sea. Along the way from Sabarmati to Dandi, many marchers joined him, and 24 days later, the group started making salt from evaporated seawater.

The Salt March launched a national movement of civil disobedience. Approximately 60,000 Indians were jailed for violating the Salt Acts, including Gandhi, who was imprisoned in May 1930. The protests elevated Gandhi into an international figure. *Time* magazine named him their Man of the Year for 1930. Neither this worldwide recognition nor imprisonment by the British affected Gandhi, and he remained tranquil while doing his duty to make India independent.

The British government launched the London Round Table Conference on Indian Constitutional Reform in August 1931, with Gandhi in attendance as the sole representative of the Indian National Congress. The conference, however, proved fruitless. He embarked on a six-day fast to protest the British decision to consider those on the lowest rung of India's caste system, called the untouchables, as a separate electorate group. The British amended the proposal. Gandhi left the leadership of the Indian National Congress in 1934, and it passed on to Jawaharlal Nehru.

As Britain found itself engulfed in World War II in 1942, Gandhi launched the Quit India movement, which called for the immediate British withdrawal from the country. In August 1942, the government arrested Gandhi and his family along with several leaders of the Indian National Congress. To justify his crackdown in India, Prime Minister Winston Churchill told British Parliament that "I have not become the King's First Minister in order to preside at the liquidation of the British Empire." With his health failing, Gandhi was released from prison in 1944 after 19 months.

After the Labour Party won in the British General Election of 1945, it began negotiations for Indian independence with the Indian National Congress and Mohammad Ali Jinnah's Muslim League. Gandhi played an active role in the negotiations and tried hard for a unified India. However, the final plan called for the partition of India along religious lines into two independent states—a predominantly Hindu India and a predominantly Muslim Pakistan. Even under this blow to his dream of a unified India, Gandhi remained tranquil and hoped that the Hindus and Muslims would live peacefully with each other after the partition.

Today, Gandhi's dream is mostly fulfilled in India, with over 200 million Muslims (some 15 percent of its population) living peacefully with Indian Hindus. Muslims also occupy the country's highest offices and are leaders of the film industry and many other segments of India's business.

Pakistan was formed on August 14 and India on August 15 of 1947. Violence between Hindus and Muslims spread in different parts of India, as Gandhi had predicted. As the killings multiplied, Gandhi toured riot-torn areas in an appeal for peace and fasted in an attempt to end the bloodshed. Some Hindus, however, increasingly viewed Gandhi as a traitor for expressing sympathy toward Muslims. This would eventually lead to his assassination on January 30, 1948.

The 78-year-old Gandhi was shot and killed by a Hindu extremist, Nathuram Godse, who was upset at Gandhi's tolerance of Muslims. During the regular late-afternoon prayer meeting that was held in New Delhi, Godse knelt before Gandhi and shot him at point-blank range with a semiautomatic pistol. The violent act took the life of a pacifist who had spent his life preaching nonviolence. Godse and his coconspirator were executed by hanging in November 1949. Additional conspirators were sentenced to life in prison.

Gandhi's life gives us several lessons in what it takes to be tranquil under the most trying circumstances, even as a political prisoner for holding and acting on your principles of nonviolence (Ahimsa) and peaceful independence for an oppressed population of over 500 million. The lessons are:

- Have a firm faith in scriptures and the power of God's will. Many of us want immediate results for our actions and are not patient to wait for God's will. We tend to take shortcuts or resort to unjust or unethical practices to reach our goal in a short time. Alternatively, we may become depressed or suffer other mental issues that affect both ourselves and those dear to us. This lesson can help us rely on the scriptures to guide us in our daily activities.

- Be disciplined and embrace the principles and virtues of a values-based life described in this book. Do your duty diligently and be patient for the results of your work, even if they take decades—like Gandhi, who waited for over 33 years after reaching India from South Africa.

- Live a simple life and reduce your wants. This will lead to less desire for material comforts, and you can be satisfied with modest needs that help you lead a healthy and peaceful life. Gandhi sacrificed all his comforts to understand the plight of the poor in India and fought relentlessly for their just place in society. When we live a simple life, we minimize our carbon footprint and live in harmony with the environment.

- Be relentless in pursuit of your goals while remaining tranquil on a day-to-day basis. Gandhi demonstrated this every day of his life. He fought against a huge and powerful foreign adversary while remaining true to his message of nonviolence and never losing faith in the people he led.

Nelson Mandela

I chose Nelson Mandela because of his leadership and tranquility even under the harsh imprisonment by the South African government that he endured for 27 years. Nelson Mandela's original name included the Xhosa name Rolihlahla, which literally means "pulling the branch of a tree" but in common usage means "troublemaker." Mandela was a South African lawyer who is surely most widely remembered for relentlessly fighting against apartheid, the system of discrimination and segregation in South Africa that subjugated the country's nonwhite population to its white minority.

Nelson Mandela was born on July 18, 1918, in the village of Mvezo to the tribal chief of the Thembu people. His father died when Nelson was 12, and the young boy was raised by the Thembu regent, Jongintaba, in Mqhekezweni. He finished his high school education at Healdtown, taking a particular interest in African history.

At the age of 21, Mandela entered the South African Native College (later the University of Fort Hare), the only degree-granting center of higher education for nonwhite people in the country. In 1940 his studies were interrupted when he was expelled for taking part in a student protest. When he returned to Mqhekezweni, however, Mandela found that Jongintaba was so angry at his dismissal that he and a cousin ran away to Johannesburg. While working there, he began attending African National Congress (ANC) meetings, developing his interest in politics. He also began his studies again and by 1942 had completed coursework through the University of South Africa sufficient for his BA. In 1943 Mandela returned to the University of Fort Hare and graduated. That same year, Mandela returned to Johannesburg to become a lawyer. He also began studies at the University of Witwatersrand for his LLD. Mandela was the only Black student at the Wits, and although he suffered racial discrimination, he managed to become a friend with many European liberals and communists, as well as with Jews and Hindus.

In October 1944, Mandela married Evelyn Mase, an ANC activist from Engcobo, who was studying to become a nurse. They would have two sons, Madiba "Thembi" Thembekile and Makgatho, and two daughters, both named Makaziwe (one of whom died in infancy). Mandela helped found the ANC Youth League, with Oliver Tambo and Walter Sisulu, to promote racial equality. A year later, he would become general secretary and two years later, president. In 1952 Nelson Mandela led the Defiance Campaign, urging Black people to violate laws of racial segregation. He was found guilty under the law against Communism and was banned from attending meetings or leaving the Johannesburg area. He passed the exams to become a lawyer and, together with Tambo, he founded one of the first Black law firms in the country. At an early age, he showed exceptional leadership and entrepreneurship, both of which would serve him well in politics.

On June 26, 1955, the Congress Alliance, a coalition of the ANC and other anti-apartheid groups, adopted the Freedom Charter, a document drafted in secrecy that demanded a democratic, free, and egalitarian society in South Africa. On December 5, 1956, Mandela was among some 150 people arrested and put on trial for high treason. By March 1961, last of the Freedom Charter defendants were finally acquitted of the treason charges. During the long course of the so-called Treason Trial, however, much activity continued. On the personal front, in 1958 Mandela divorced wife Evelyn and married social worker Winnie Madik-izela, with whom he would have two daughters, Zenani and Zindziswa. In 1961 he went underground and helped create Umkhonto weSizwe (Spear of the Nation), an armed wing of the ANC, becoming their leader. A year later, he left South Africa and attended the Pan-African confer-ence in Addis Ababa. He received guerrilla training there and elsewhere in Africa, and then went to London seeking further support for the armed struggle. When he returned to South Africa, he was arrested and sentenced to five years in prison for illegal abandonment of his country.

In October 1963, following a police raid in the suburb of Rivonia on a secret Umkhonto weSizwe headquarters filled with arms and equip-ment, Mandela was taken to join 10 of his compatriots to be tried for sabotage under threat of the death penalty. In the course of what became known as the Rivonia Trial, Mandela made what would become endur-ingly known as his "Speech from the Dock," on April 20, 1964. Toward the end of that speech are these words:

> I have fought against white domination, and I have
> fought against black domination. I have cherished
> the ideal of a democratic and free society in which
> all persons live together in harmony and with equal
> opportunities. It is an ideal which I hope to live for
> and to achieve. But if needs be, it is an ideal for which
> I am prepared to die.[27]

This conviction to give his life for his country helped him survive many years of imprisonment and constantly work for a racially inclusive South Africa.

On June 12, 1964, a judge found Mandela and other activists guilty and sentenced them to life imprisonment. All but one (the sole white defendant) were sent to Robben Island, where they remained for 18 years.

Mandela was confined to a damp cell, with horrible living conditions. Despite being in prison, Mandela was visited by well-known South African leaders because of his political activism. The prison conditions improved, and he was given better quality food. During all the trials and tribulations in his life, he remained calm and charmed the prison guards with his kindness and concern for his fellow prisoners. By 1975 he was considered a Class A prisoner, which allowed him to have many visits, receive correspondence, and study. He wrote his autobiography and remained involved in South African politics. He secretly sent it to London, and although it was not published for several years, the authorities found several written pages of his book and took away his privilege

---

27 Nelson Mandela, *The Historic Speech of Nelson Rolihlahla Mandela at the Rivonia Trial : As Delivered from the Dock on April 20, 1964* (Learn & Teach Publications, 1988).

to study for four years. He was not discouraged but devoted his time to gardening and reading, until he resumed his legal work in 1980.

In 1973, with significant pressure from the United States and other countries, the United Nations (UN) declared the policy of apartheid a crime against humanity. In 1981 South African journalist Percy Qoboza launched the slogan "Free Mandela," which prompted an international campaign for his release led by the UN Security Council. In April 1982, Mandela was transferred to Pollsmoor prison in Tokai, a suburb of Cape Town. The conditions of the prison were better, although Mandela missed the companionship of many of the prisoners and guards in Robben Island, as well as the natural space of the island itself.

On December 12, 1988, Mandela was taken to Tygerberg hospital for having fallen ill with tuberculosis. Once he recovered, he was transferred to Victor Verster prison, which had better conditions. On February 11, 1990, after 27 years in prison, he was released, and on March 2 of the same year, he was elected vice president of the ANC. By June 17, 1991, after more than four decades, the South African parliament repealed the laws on racial segregation of the population. Mandela proved that through patience and persistence, and by maintaining his inner tranquility, he could defeat the worst impulses of the apartheid supporters.

On July 6, 1991, Mandela was elected president of the ANC by acclamation and became the successor of Oliver Tambo. In 1993 he shared the Nobel Prize for Peace with President F. W. de Klerk of South Africa. All this recognition of Mandela, as well as the worldwide call to end apartheid, prompted President de Klerk to hold the first free election in the country on April 26, 1994. Twenty million citizens exercised their right to vote for the first time, ending more than three hundred years of white domination. On May 10, 1994, with 62.6 percent of the vote, Nelson Mandela became the first Black president in the history of South Africa.

Mandela initiated a reconstruction and development program to improve the living standards of Black South Africans in areas of education, housing, health, and employment. In 1994 his autobiography, *Long Walk to Freedom*,[28] was published. Mandela promoted a new constitution for the country that finally was adopted by the Parliament in 1996. In March 1999, suffering from prostate cancer, he said goodbye to the Parliament, naming Thabo Mbeki as the new president to succeed him. When he retired from political life in June 1999, he dedicated himself to the promotion of various humanitarian causes. In 2003 the Mandela Foundation launched a major international campaign to raise funds to fight against Acquired Immune Deficiency Syndrome (AIDS) that was killing many in Africa. President George W. Bush joined this effort by pledging $15 billion to help in the global fight against AIDS. The emphasis was on access to life-saving treatment and care for millions of people in Africa and the Caribbean.

In 2008 the world celebrated Mandela's 90th birthday with an appeal for peace. London paid tribute to him with a macro concert. A year later, the UN declared July 18th as his International Day. In 2010, on the 20th anniversary of his release from prison, he published *Conversations with Myself*. After suffering a prolonged respiratory infection, Mandela died on December 5, 2013, at the age of 95 at his home in Houghton, Johannesburg. He was surrounded by his family and friends, after having lived a life of major accomplishments for his country and the world. Before he died, he said, "Death is something inevitable. When a man has done what he considers his duty to his

---

28 Nelson Mandela, *Long Walk to Freedom: The Autobiography of Nelson Mandela* (Little, Brown, 1994).

people and his country, he can rest in peace. I believe that I have made that effort and that is, therefore, why I will sleep for the eternity."

Few men have changed the course of history as Nelson Mandela did. He was a tireless fighter and is considered a global symbol of freedom and hope who, despite spending 27 years in prison, managed to defeat the racist regime of apartheid, one of the most ruthless of the 20th century. He was the first democratic president of South Africa and helped usher in the end of officially sanctioned racial segregation in his country through a process of reconciliation and social justice.

A few of the awards he received include:

- Lenin Peace Prize in 1990, presented by the Soviet Union
- Bharat Ratna in 1990, presented by the Indian government
- Honorary Member of the Order of Merit in 1995, presented by Queen Elizabeth II
- Nobel Prize for Peace in 1993, presented by the Nobel Foundation

Nelson Mandela's life of tranquility under the harsh conditions of being a political prisoner for fighting for the rights of Black and other nonwhite South Africans teaches many lessons about how we can live our life. Among these lessons are:

- Live a life of faith, believing in the Christian value of tolerance toward one's oppressors. This faith propelled him to fight against apartheid, a system that Mahatma Gandhi fought against when living in South Africa. This allowed him to initiate the Truth and Reconciliation Commission in

South Africa, and to never take revenge against the people who had oppressed him throughout his adult life.

- Never lose hope, even under extremely harsh treatment by authorities, and fight for freedom your people against all odds. Mandela believed strongly that justice will prevail and that the apartheid system would be dismantled.

- Persevere until your goal is reached. Although he was imprisoned several times, the longest period being 27 years, which would have broken many people, he never lost sight of his goal and he worked to build the ANC, which provided many young leaders to continue fighting for justice.

- Put public interest above self-interest. This is one lesson he demonstrated throughout his life. And it would be an excellent lesson for the politicians of today who put their self-interest (of winning the next election) above the public interest.

Barack Obama

Barack Obama was a choice of mine for the self-confidence and tranquility he exuded throughout his political career, working against immense odds to become the first Black president of the United States and winning a second term for his leadership of the people. He served as president from 2009 to 2016.

Barack Hussein Obama was born on August 4, 1961, and from very ordinary circumstances rose to become the leader of the free world with the faith he had in the goodness of the people of the United States. His father, Obama Sr., was an international student from Kenya, and his mother was Stanley Ann Dunham of Kansas. He was born and grew up in Hawaii, mostly under the guidance of his mother and grandparents. He graduated from Punahou School in Honolulu in 1979 and got his undergraduate degree from Columbia University, New York, in 1983. Leaving a well-paying job in New York City, he devoted three years of his life to working with the Developing Communities Project in the poorest sections of the South Side of Chicago. His efforts raised the project's annual budget from $70,000 to over $400,000. In 1988 he enrolled in Harvard Law School, where he would serve as president of the prestigious *Harvard Law Review*. After graduation, instead of taking a lucrative offer from a law firm, he decided to return to Chicago and work in civil rights. His mother had instilled him the values that she saw in the Civil Rights Movement: tolerance, equality, and standing up for the disadvantaged.

In 1992 Obama married Michelle Robinson, a young lawyer in the Chicago law firm in which he had earlier been a summer associate. He and Michelle have two daughters, Malia Ann and Natasha (Sasha). Also that year, he joined the University of Chicago as a professor of constitutional law and was very active in Project Vote, where he registered over 150,000 African American voters. In 1995 Obama wrote his first book, *Dreams from My Father: A History of Race and Inheritance*.[29] It became a number-one *New York Times* bestseller and thrust him into politics. In 1996 he entered politics and won a seat in the Illinois State Senate. In 2004 he won a seat in the U.S. Senate. Although not well known statewide, he ran an excellent U.S. Senate campaign and won by more than 64 percent over his Republican opponent.

---

29   Barack Obama, *Dreams from My Father: A History of Race and Inheritance* (Times Books, 1995).

This impressive victory caught the attention of the national Democratic Party, and Obama was selected as one of the youngest keynote speakers at the 2004 Democratic Convention in Boston, Massachusetts. His rousing speech at the convention gave him a reputation throughout the country. In 2007 Obama announced his candidacy for U.S. president. Many thought he didn't stand a chance, but by organizing a strong grassroots campaign that garnered many small donations, he won the Democratic primary on June 3, 2008. Obama went on to win the presidency in November with a landslide victory over Senator John McCain, his Republican opponent, who was a well-known politician and veteran. In 2009 Obama was awarded the Nobel Prize for Peace for his commitment to reduce nuclear weapons worldwide.

Let's take a look at the values that made Obama's meteoric rise from state senator to U.S. senator to president of the United States possible in such a short time. In his book *The Audacity of Hope: Thoughts on Reclaiming the American Dream*,[30] he said, "Based on my experience as a Senator and lawyer, husband and father, Christian and skeptic—... we can ground our politics in the notion of a common good." He goes on to state several values that he has developed since childhood, including empathy, self-reliance and self-improvement, risk-taking, drive, discipline, temperance, and hard work. Other values listed by Obama include:

- Community, caring for others in our groups, however defined
- Patriotism, which includes the obligations of citizenship, a sense of duty, and sacrifice on behalf of the nation

---

30 Barack Obama, *The Audacity of Hope: Thoughts on Reclaiming the American Dream* (Crown Publishers, 2006).

- Faith in something bigger than ourselves, which includes religion and ethics
- Honesty
- Fairness
- Humility
- Kindness
- Courtesy
- Compassion

Obama's concern for the common good and for equitable treatment of minorities in the United States was a major factor in his appeal to a majority of Americans who voted for his presidency in both 2008 and 2012. He brought the message of hope to millions of Americans and Muslims around the world, and emphasized the reduction of nuclear weapons and raw materials in countries that have or can make nuclear weapons. His faith is a key factor in working for social change in the U.S. and for changing a large portion of the economy that is responsible for the health and welfare of the population. In his role as a community organizer in Chicago, he said in *The Audacity of Hope,* "In the day-to-day work of the men and women I met in church each day, in their ability to 'make a way out of no way' and maintain hope and dignity in the direst of circumstances, I could see the Word made manifest." He said that his work with pastors and laypeople in Chicago deepened his resolve to lead a public life, and it fortified his racial identity while confirming his belief in the capacity of ordinary people to do extraordinary things. He saw the equal value of all people and was the first president to support marriage between gay couples and to work to ensure that there should be no discrimination with regard to sexual orientation.

Obama also stresses opportunity in *The Audacity of Hope*. He believes strongly that education, science and technology, and energy independence will make the United States competitive and strong, and he provided massive government resources to achieve these opportunities for the American people. He brought together 190 countries from around the world to agree on a framework for managing climate change when the Paris Agreement was signed in 2015. He was instrumental in achieving significant funding for new solar technologies in the U.S. and helped make solar technology competitive with other energy sources.

In addition, Obama went to poor communities lacking opportunity and underscored to them the primary responsibility of parents to instill an ethic of hard work and educational achievement in their children. He promoted early childhood education for every child, rigorous curriculum with emphasis on math, science and literacy skills, and the recruitment and training of transformative principals and more effective teachers. Obama forged a partnership between government, business, and workers to accelerate innovation and improve wages for workers in manufacturing and other sectors of the economy. The first piece of legislation he signed was the Equality of Wages for Women.

Among the many positive effects that highlight Obama's tenure as president, his landmark accomplishment has to have been the Affordable Care Act, which passed with exclusively Democratic support. He strongly believed that through increased preventive care and lower administrative and malpractice costs, a subsidy could be provided to low-income American individuals and families who wanted to purchase a medical plan through state insurance pools. For the first time, previously existing health-care conditions were not sufficient reason for an insurance company to refuse an individual medical coverage. The Affordable Care Act (colloquially known as Obamacare) was able to provide insurance to an additional 20 million Americans, mostly from low-income families.

Throughout his presidency, Obama maintained the prestige of American values around the world, and under his leadership, countries worldwide came to a comprehensive agreement to reduce greenhouse gas emissions. His efforts at promoting renewable energy in the United States reduced the price of those resources, and his push for a cleaner environment has improved air quality in many cities. Many of poor were provided opportunity through federal government programs, and he reduced the level of poverty in minority communities around the country.

His permanent legacy for the country is the Obama Presidential Center that, at the time of writing, is being built in Chicago, adjacent to the University of Chicago campus. The project aims, too, at revitalizing the city's South Side, which has an inordinately large number of poor minorities struggling to improve their lives. It will be both a world-class museum and a public gathering space that celebrates the nation's first African American president and first lady. The center will represent the vision of Barack and Michelle Obama for the world, and will be an inspiration for future generations of Black and underprivileged youth to hope and work for a better future.

The characteristics that made Obama successful as the first African American president of the United States and kept him tranquil through the challenging eight years of his administration can be summed up as follows:

- His faith in himself and the people he worked with in the South Side of Chicago, and the ability of people to have hope under the most difficult situations.
- His ability to work with diverse groups of Americans and find common ground from which to approach the fundamental problems facing people.
- His strong connection to family and the sense of purpose that drove him to aim for and achieve the seemingly impossible.
- His vision for a brighter future with equity and justice for everyone, irrespective of their color, creed, or economic status.
- His global vision of a world where nuclear materials should not proliferate.
- His vision of the oneness of humanity, which made him strive for the removal of barriers to the enjoyment of the freedoms enshrined in the U.S. Constitution.

Mother Teresa

Mother Teresa—now formally Saint Teresa of Calcutta—presented a model choice for me as an inspirational leader, for her faith in the presence of God in the poorest people of India and for her tranquility through many years of struggle to establish her Missionaries of Charity in India and other parts of the world.

Mother Teresa was born Agnes Gonxha Bojaxhiu on August 26, 1910, in Skopje, Macedonia. When she died at the age of 87 in Calcutta (now Kolkata), she was given a national funeral and acknowledged worldwide for her charitable work for the poorest people of Kolkata and her leadership in the Missionaries of Charity, the Roman Catholic religious order she founded that, in the first quarter of the 21st century, had over 5,000 nuns and was active in more than 133 coun-tries. She was beatified on October 19, 2003, in Saint Peter's Square, Vatican City, by Pope John Paul II, and canonized by Pope Francis I on September 4, 2016. How did a woman born to a humble ethnic Albanian parents become such a revered hero of the poor? How did she retain her tranquility and qualities of compassion for her fellow human beings under such trying situations in a country far away from where she was born?

For 18 years, Teresa lived in Skopje before she moved to Ireland to join the Sisters of Loreto, and then almost immediately to India, where she lived her life of service until her death in 1997. She arrived in India in 1929 and began her novitiate in Darjeeling, in the lower Himalayas, where she learned Bengali and taught at St. Teresa's School near her convent. Teresa took her solemn vows in May 1937, while she was a teacher at the Loreto Convent in Entally, eastern Kolkata. She served there for nearly 20 years and was appointed its headmistress in 1944. Although she enjoyed teaching, she was disturbed by the poverty surrounding her in Kolkata, and the Bengal famine of 1943 brought even deeper misery and death to the city.

In 1946 Mother Teresa heard the call of her innermost conscience, which she described as the "call within the call." She felt she should serve the poor by staying with them, so she asked for and received permission to leave the school. Her missionary work started in 1948, and she spent several months in Patna to receive basic medical train-ing at Holy Family Hospital. After this, she ventured into the slums to understand the poverty of slum dwellers. She founded a school in Motijhil, Kolkata, before she began tending to the poor and hungry. At the beginning of 1949, she was joined in her effort by a group of young women, and she laid the foundation for a new religious community helping the "poorest among the poor." She founded that organization in 1950 as the Missionaries of Charity. Mother Teresa wore a sari with a blue border, wrapped in Bengali style, as do all nuns of the order.

Mother Teresa's efforts quickly caught the attention of Indian officials, including Prime Minister Jawaharlal Nehru. Her first year was full of difficulty, and with no income, she begged for food and supplies. She experienced doubt and loneliness, and was tempted to return to the comfort of convent life during these early months. She resisted the temptations and decided only to serve the poor. On October 7, 1950, she received official Vatican permission for the diocesan congregation, which would become the Missionaries of Charity. The objective of the missionaries was to care for "the hungry, the naked, the homeless, the crippled, the blind, the lepers, all those people who feel unwanted, unloved, uncared for throughout society, people that have become a burden to the society and are shunned by everyone."

In 1952 she opened her first hospice with the help of Kolkata officials. She converted an abandoned Hindu temple into Nirmal Hriday (Home for the Pure of Heart). At this place, people received medical attention and the opportunity to die with dignity in accordance with their faith: Muslims were read the Quran, Hindus received water from the River Ganges, and Catholics received extreme unction. A beautiful death, Teresa said, is for people who lived like animals to die like angels. She opened a hospice for those with leprosy, calling it Shanti Nagar (City of Peace). Her team established leprosy-outreach clinics throughout Kolkata, providing medication, dressings, and food. They took in an increasing number of homeless children; in 1955, Mother Teresa opened Nirmala Shishu Bhavan, the Children's Home for the Immaculate Heart, as a haven for orphans and homeless youth. The congregation began to attract recruits and donations, and by the 1960s, it had hospices, orphanages, and leper houses throughout India. Teresa expanded the congregation abroad, opening a house in Venezuela with five sisters in 1965. Houses followed in Italy (Rome), Tanzania, and Austria in 1968, and during the 1970s, the congregation opened houses and foundations in the United States and dozens of countries in Asia, Africa, and Europe.

The Missionaries of Charity Brothers was founded in 1963, and a contemplative branch of the sisters followed in 1976. Many priests requested her to expand her operations, and in 1981, she founded the Corpus Christi Movement for Priests and, with Joseph Langford, the Missionaries of Charity Fathers in 1984. These organizations combined the vocational aims of the Missionaries of Charity with the resources of the priesthood. By 1997 the 13-member Kolkata congregation had grown to more than 4,000 sisters who managed orphanages, AIDS hospices, and charity centers worldwide, caring for refugees, the blind, disabled, aged, alcoholics, the poor and homeless, and victims of floods, epidemics, and famine. By 2007 the Missionaries of Charity numbered about 450 brothers and 5,000 sisters worldwide, operating 600 missions, schools, and shelters in 120 countries.

Mother Teresa said, "By blood, I am Albanian, by citizenship, an Indian, and by faith, a Catholic nun. As to my calling, I belong to the world. As to my heart, I belong to the Heart of Jesus." She was fluent in five languages: Bengali, Albanian, Serbian, English, and Hindi. At the height of the siege in Beirut in 1982, she rescued 37 children trapped in a frontline hospital by brokering a temporary cease-fire between the Israeli army and the Palestinian guerillas. Accompanied by Red Cross workers, she traveled through the war zone to the hospital to evacuate the children.

When Eastern Europe experienced increased openness in the late 1980s, Mother Teresa expanded her efforts to Communist countries, which had rejected the Missionaries of Charity. She began dozens of projects, undeterred by criticism of her stands against abortion and divorce. "No matter who says what, you should accept it with a smile and do your own work." She visited Armenia after the 1988 earthquake and met with Soviet Premier Nikolai Ryzhkov. She traveled to assist the hungry in Ethiopia, radiation victims at Chernobyl, and earthquake victims in Armenia. In 1991 she returned to Albania for the first time and opened a Missionaries of Charity Brothers home in Tirana. The first Missionaries of Charity home in the United States was established in the south Bronx area of New York City, and by 1984, the congregation operated 19 centers throughout the United States.

Mother Teresa had a heart attack in Rome in 1983, while she was visiting Pope John Paul II. Following a second heart attack in 1989, she received a pacemaker. In 1991 she had further heart problems and wanted to resign as head of the Missionaries of Charity. However, the sisters voted for her to stay and continue the work. On March 13, 1997, she resigned as head of the organization, and she died on September 5, 1997. At the time of her death, the Missionaries of Charity had over 4,000 sisters and an associated brotherhood of 300 members, operating 610 missions in 123 countries. They were aided by coworkers numbering over one million.

Mother Teresa lay in repose in an open casket in St. Thomas Church, Kolkata, for a week before her funeral. She received a state funeral from the Indian government in gratitude for her service to the poor of all religions in the country. According to the former UN Secretary-General Javier Perez de Cuellar, "She is the United Nations. She is peace in the world."

Her recognitions and awards included the following:

- The Padma Shri in 1962, by the Indian government
- The Jawaharlal Nehru Award for International Understanding in 1969, by the Indian government
- The Bharat Ratna (India's highest civilian award) in 1980
- A special Rs. 5 coin, minted in her honor by the Indian government in 2010
- The Ramon Magsaysay Award for Peace and International Understanding in 1962
- The Pope John XXIII Peace Prize in 1971
- The Companion of the Order of Australia in 1982
- The Order of Merit in 1983 by the United Kingdom
- The Albert Schweitzer International Prize in 1975
- The Nobel Prize for Peace in 1979

Mother Teresa's life shows how one person can bring her inner tranquility and determination to bear to conquer seemingly unyielding obstacles and overwhelming situations. She was steadfast in her caring for the poor and those rejected by society, and she spread her message of kindness and service to all parts of the world. The main lessons we can learn are:

- Embrace a purpose early in your life and pursue it relentlessly, against all odds. Mother Teresa could have lived a life of comfort in the convent, but she could not endure the sight of the lepers and other poor people rejected by society through no fault of their own.

- Persevere under difficult circumstances to achieve your purpose. In her initial years in Kolkata, her desire to help the poor was met with great skepticism in India, a land she adopted after leaving her home in Macedonia. But her determination convinced the Vatican to allow her to start the Missionaries of Charity in Kolkata and the Kolkata government to give her assistance in her work.

- She saw humanity in human suffering and believed in the universality of religions. She administered Hindu rites to Hindus (who died in her care), Muslim rites to Muslims, and Christian rites to Christians. This oneness of vision is required to have compassion for all and to do your best for your fellow human beings.

- Mother Teresa expanded her work throughout the world since she didn't see geographical boundaries but rather the unbounded suffering of humanity wherever she looked. She was unafraid to speak out about the conditions of the poor and fearless about mobilizing support from individuals and governments to alleviate human suffering.

Warren Buffett

I chose Warren Buffett as an inspirational leader from the turbulent world of business and finance not just because of the calmness he embodies in that world but also for the empathy he has proven for his fellow human beings. Buffett has made billions of dollars, much of it through his famed talent for investing, and has decided to give 99 percent of his fortune to charities, such as the Bill and Melinda Gates Foundation, that make an enormous difference in the quality of life for so many people around the world.

Warren Buffett was born in Omaha, Nebraska, on August 30, 1930. He learned in high school how to be successful with money and later wanted to drop out of college, but his congressman father, Howard Buffett, encouraged him to get a college degree. Young Buffett started his undergraduate work at the University of Pennsylvania but finished at the University of Nebraska. He was fascinated by the work of Columbia University's Professor Benjamin Graham in stock analysis and value investing, and Buffett finished a master's degree at Columbia in 1954. Graham's basic philosophy of investing, which is still followed by many around the world, was "look at stocks as business, use the market's fluctuations to your advantage, and seek a margin of safety." Buffett said that was what he learned from Benjamin Graham. "A hundred years from now, they will still be the cornerstones of investing."

Buffett has long been called the *Oracle of Omaha*. In 1956, he started the Buffett Partnership. In 1962, Buffett's company began aggressively purchasing shares of Berkshire Hathaway, a company in the textiles business, and by 1965, it owned a controlling interest. With this takeover, Buffett began divesting Berkshire Hathaway of its textiles holdings. In 1970, he changed the name of Buffett Partnership to Berkshire Hathaway Diversified Holding Company, and by 1985, he had closed all the textile mills that were not profitable. He focused his holdings in insurance, newspapers, media (e.g., ABC Capital Cities), finance (e.g., Salomon Brothers), and consumer product companies (Coca-Cola). Having become a millionaire in 1962 (at the age of 32), he became a billionaire in 1990. He did this in part by associating with exceptionally gifted people like his professor Benjamin Graham and his longtime partner at Berkshire Hathaway, Charles Munger. As of 2008, Warren Buffett was the world's richest person, with a personal value of $62 billion.

During the financial crisis in 2008–2009, Buffett remarked that "very few people could appreciate the bubble of 2008–2009. That is the nature of bubbles. They are mass delusions." However, he survived the crisis without much loss since his holding company had a diversified portfolio of companies. Presidential candidate Barack Obama met with him in 2008 and was impressed with Buffett's simplicity and wisdom. In 2011, President Obama gave him the Presidential Medal of Freedom.

Buffet is a sought-after speaker and advises both institutional and individual investors. During his career, Buffett has capped his own salary at $100,000, whereas many CEOs earn salaries in the millions of dollars, not including their stock bonuses and other perks of their position. In 2007 *Time* magazine selected him as one of the year's 100 Most Influential People. And in 2009, Buffett was elected to the American Philosophical Society.

Warren Buffett has been perhaps equally famous for his philanthropy. He gave $50 million to the Nuclear Threat Initiative, a nonpartisan, nonprofit global security organization focused on reducing the nuclear and biological threats imperiling the world. He has given a majority of his funds to the Bill and Melinda Gates Foundation for their global work on health and development in many parts of the world. He auctions a lunch with himself once a year to raise money for charities that were close to him and his late first wife, Susie. His daughter, also named Susie, does charitable work through the Susan A. Buffett Foundation. In 2016 he started www.drive2vote. com, a website to encourage people to exercise their right to vote, as well as to assist in registering voters and to arrange to drive them to a polling place if they needed a ride. In 2018 his company joined JPMorgan Chase and Amazon to form a health care company for their U.S. employees. These activities demonstrate his civic and moral sense of his obligations to society for the wealth he has earned with his business skills. Very few businesspeople can claim anything close to such an exemplary record of public service.

Buffett has retained his simple ways of living and has been an example to many students and investors around the world. His philanthropy includes starting the Giving Pledge in 2009, along with Bill Gates, through which he has urged many millionaires and billionaires to share at least 50 percent of their wealth for humanitarian causes. He has influenced many in business and government, including President Barack Obama. Buffett exemplifies the best of capitalism, representing it as a system in which wealth is created in society and used to uplift the lives of ordinary citizens. One of his most famous quotations is this: "We have learned to turn out lots of goods and services, but we haven't learned as well how to have everybody share in the bounty. The obligation of a society as prosperous as ours is to figure out how nobody gets left too far behind."

The reasons Warren Buffett achieved success while keeping tranquil in the volatile world of Wall Street include the following:

- Self-confidence in his abilities from a young age

- Consistency in his method of investing over a long period of time
- Concern for his fellow human beings and the willingness to share his wealth with others less fortunate
- Living a simple life and never being carried away by his success in the financial world
- A strong sense of morals and responsibility to community and family
- Mentoring many in the financial world and sharing his knowledge generously with others
- Teaching his children the value of hard work and of relying on themselves

A. P. J. Abdul Kalam

I chose to include Kalam because, although he was born into a modest fisherman family, he rose to become president of India, influencing the lives of millions of youth throughout the country. He became a role model to young scientists in particular and launched India into the Space Age.

Kalam was born Avul Pakir Jainulabdeen Abdul Kalam on October 15, 1931, in Rameswaram, India, and died of a sudden heart attack on July 27, 2015, in Shillong, India. He was a greatly beloved figure in India and represented the opportunity and diversity in the country. I had the unique opportunity to meet him at the Indian Science Congress in 2005, and his address to the gathering was electrifying. He rushed off from this assembly as he had an appointment with the youth from the National Design Institute in the city of Ahmedabad, where our conference was being held. He loved meeting with the youth of India and had set himself a goal of meeting 500,000 young people one-on-one throughout the land.

Kalam was born into a fisherman's family on the southeast coast of India. He was a devout Muslim and a good student, and he graduated from the Madras Institute of Technology as an aeronautical engineer, joining the Defence Research and Development Organization (DRDO) after that. Kalam worked on missile technologies and joined the Indian Space Research Organization (ISRO) when it was formed. In 1980 he was responsible for the first successful launch of the Satellite Launch Vehicle, namely the SLV-III, which was designed and produced in India using technologies developed at DRDO and ISRO. He was also responsible for the development of the Polar Satellite Launch Vehicle (PSLV). From 1982 until his election as president of India in 2002, he was the director of DRDO. In that position, he was responsible for the program that developed a number of India's missiles, including its integrated guided missiles, earning him the epithet *Missile Man*. For his scientific and technological work, Kalam was recognized by the U.S. National Aeronautics and Space Administration's (NASA) Jet Propulsion Laboratory when it named a new bacterium found in the International Space Station for him: *Solibacillus kalamii*.

Kalam's simplicity and his love of science and promoting the study of science among the youth made him a national hero who was loved by all segments of society, Muslims and Hindus alike. His work on developing India's space industry and taking charge of making indigenous technology capable of producing India's first nuclear bomb made him a national hero. He was sought after by many institutions in India to inspire the country's youth to dream big and achieve India's full potential.

Although he was a practicing Muslim, Kalam was well versed in the Hindu tradition and scriptures. He embodied the spirit of syncretism, the appreciation of various elements of different spiritual and cultural traditions. He was a unifier of diverse traditions and worked hard for a united India. He learned Sanskrit, the language of the Hindu scriptures, and read the main text of the Hindu scriptures. He worked with Pramukh Swami, the leader of BAPS, a Hindu denomination that is dedicated to human development and peace.

One of Kalam's final books was *Transcendence: My Spiritual Experiences with Pramukh Swamiji.*[31] He loved writing Tamil poetry and playing the veena, an ancient musical instrument of India. He also loved technology, of course, and what it has been able to do and could still achieve for the betterment of people of all economic backgrounds in India. His book *India 2020*[32] presented a detailed blueprint for India to become a developed country by the year 2020, outlining how the benefits of technology might be available to the advantage of all India's citizens.

After his term as president, Kalam taught at several management universities in India and was active in social causes. In 2011 he started the What Can I Give movement in India to foster the spirit of social service throughout the country. In 2012 he created a handheld tablet for use by medical personnel in remote rural areas, an action that facilitated the provision of medical services to the poor in those Indian regions. For his efforts to promote the development of youth, the Indian government declared October 15th, his birthday, to be Youth Renaissance Day. Other awards bestowed on Kalam by the Indian government include:

---

31 A. P. J. Abdul Kalam, *Transcendence: My Spiritual Experiences with Pramukh Swamiji* (Harper Element, 2015).
32 A. P. J. Abdul Kalam, *India 2020: A Vision for the New Millennium* (Penguin Books India, 1998).

- The Padma Bhushan in 1981
- The Padma Vibhushan in 1990
- The Bharat Ratna, the highest civilian award, in 1997

The characteristics that made Dr. Kalam a beloved citizen of India and a leader of global peace are essentially the same as should be sought by those who wish to follow a path to tranquility in the turbulent 21st century:

- Faith in God, and in his own goal of helping every citizen of India, irrespective of class, creed, or economic status
- Belief in the human benefits of technology and working hard with perseverance to achieve his passions
- Love of country and science, and of his fellow human beings
- Seeing the oneness of humanity, and that all faiths lead to One God
- Seeing young people as the future of humanity, and spending real time guiding and inspiring them to be their best

CONCLUSIONS

There are only two mistakes one can make along the road to truth:
not going all the way, and not starting.
— THE BUDDHA

IT HAS BEEN A PERSONAL JOURNEY in writing this book based on my interest in tranquility from a young age. I was searching for it when I was 14 and tried to find the meaning of work and its reward when I was in high school. I had studied hard to get high marks in my final exams in my first year of high school and was disappointed with the results. I had scored well but not as well as I'd expected. I was disturbed that all my hard work had not helped me qualify for engineering college. My elder brother then advised me that engineering was not the only career option and that I could continue college and become a scientist. He also suggested that I balance my academic work with some exercise and fun. I thought about his counsel and started doing just that: I began studying for my bachelor of science in math, physics, and geology.

I did well with that new direction and had fun in life, and I started to realize that I should not expect immediate gratification from my work. I worked hard for two years, and when I was 16, I applied to the local engineering college with the marks I had obtained when I was 14. I also attached other qualifications I had obtained in the two years since then. Lo and behold, I was called in for an interview and given a seat in engineering college. I was thrilled and joined the engineering college since I was still interested in being an engineer.

That year was an eye-opener for me. I realized that I will be rewarded for my work, but not when I want it: when I should get it. From that time on, my thinking changed and I simply did my best and left the results to the will of God, our Higher Being. That God runs the whole universe and has given us the laws by which the natural ecosystems operate. I stopped worrying about influencing the outcomes of my work, and I was instead confident that I would get what I deserved. The effect of this change in my perspective was to shift the burden off of me, leaving me stress-free and able to enjoy life fully. I made friends, participated in university sports, and studied well.

After that time, I was able to move to the United States for graduate study in 1970, and I've subsequently enjoyed a remarkable career of over 44 years. Since retirement, I've been thinking of sharing my experience of becoming stress-free and living happily. I was prompted by my daughter, who reminded me of how I advised her during school and college to do her best and leave the rest to God. She said I should write a book on the 9 Steps I've followed to become and remain stress-free. So here is my effort to share with you how you can be stress-free by following the 9 Steps that have helped me.

Everyone Can Be Stress-Free

Stress is something we create in our mind by reacting adversely to things happening to us in our personal and professional lives. We tend to place an undue importance on success or on acquiring things we want, instead of embracing all the moments of joy that happen to us every day. I get up, take in the sunrise, and thank God for a new day filled with opportunities and surprises. This way, I set a positive tone for the entire day and accept all the coming events as new experiences I should enjoy and learn from. I generally don't get disappointed by so-called failures, but rather I consider them a learning opportunity to grow emotionally and maintain tranquility. Of course, I am affected sometimes. But I usually bounce back within a day or two, after I analyze the situation and learn from it. I have learned from my earlier experiences that everything happens for the good and it's up to me to react positively instead of negatively to whatever happens in my life. This attitude has helped me many times in my long career.

Early in my career, I was surprised by a set of events that unfolded in Vancouver, Canada. I was asked to join a company headquartered in Vancouver and told that after six months, I would be transferred to Denver and take over that office. I was excited about this opportunity and joined the company. However, the economy turned sour in the ensuing months and the company decided to close the Denver office. They told me that I had one of two options: become a Canadian immigrant and continue in Vancouver or leave the company. Since my wife was eager to start her medical practice in the United States, I told them I would leave. They gave me two months' salary, and in the first week of getting this news, I called a few friends in the United States and got an interview with a Chicago firm. I flew in and was offered the position of division manager in a small company, with the opportunity to become a partner after about three years.

So we moved to Chicago in the winter of 1982. My wife found a great practice opportunity in Chicago, and my daughter was enjoying school. However, after three years, the owner of the company informed me that he did not want me as a partner and I should find a new job. My initial reaction was "How can he promise me something and after I had proved my worth, renege on it?" I was stressed for a couple of days and, after discussing with my wife, decided to start my own company, Midwest Engineers. My company was extremely successful, and I took on challenging construction projects in the Chicago area. So what looked like a disappointment turned into an excellent professional growth opportunity that also allowed me to employ hundreds of people. Since that time, I've continued to grow professionally and been very happy with my professional and personal lives.

We all can carry guilt and hurts with us from our interactions with others, and these cause stress, which can last a long time unless we're aware of them and take steps to address them. You may not have done something that you should have done at the right time, and then later regret it and feel a sense of guilt. Many times, this guilt may just be a figment of your imagination and, when analyzed, may disappear. However, if this guilt is justified and your mind continues to bother you, just call the person whom you might have hurt in the past and apologize. Often, we feel that our sense of self can be diminished by apologizing, but I want to emphasize that this is not true, and your sense of self is enhanced when you apologize and clear your mind of this ongoing guilt.

Your inner self is your guiding light that helps you make right decisions, and it should be listened to. This can be done only when you have quiet time for yourself. So the first important thing is to ensure you have some free time every day, even for a few minutes, to analyze your emotions. You need to deal with them instead of them running you and ruining the next day. Similarly, a long-felt sense of hurt could be a figment of your imagination, and if you analyze it, you could easily forgive the person that you thought hurt you. If it persists, you should address it with the person who you think hurt you. They might have said something without thinking it through fully, and when they explain it, the hurt can disappear.

I have placed my mental peace as a high priority, next to my physical health, and I live a life of no regrets and hurts. Also, I know that my true inner self is what is constant, and the rest of the things around me constantly change. Your body goes through childhood, youth, professional life, and old age, but your inner self or the soul is ever unchanging. So abide in your inner self, and you will be stress-free and happy most of the time.

Another stressor in life comes from expecting things from others (including acknowldgment) and then becoming disappointed when they don't happen. The best way to avoid this source of stress is to drop all expectations and accept whatever happens in your life with a sense of tranquility. This advice from Swami Dayanand Saraswathi (my teacher) resonates in my mind always: "What happens to you is God's order, and mortal humans can only do what they can, the rest is up to God's will." This advice has been a source of comfort in my life, and I try to accept situations instead of trying to change them and grow disappointed. The serenity prayer is also what everyone should remember: Know what you can change and what you cannot change, and the wisdom to know the difference. If we practice this prayer and give freedom to others to be who they are, we can be mentally peaceful and stress-free. We can change only ourselves using our free will, and we cannot change others' behavior or reactions to what we say. So a stress-free life is one in which you learn from your experiences and change yourself to handle a changing world in a manner that does not disturb your inner tranquility.

Yet another class of stressor arises in the strong likes and dislikes we have developed since childhood. These mental stressors trigger things we find either highly unpleasant or greatly desired. If we have only preferences and avoid strong likes and dislikes, it is a pleasant travel through life under all circumstances that we face. Managing our likes and dislikes and making them into preferences is a lifelong process since we have built these likes and dislikes for a long time, ever since we could speak as a child. So it takes a most focused and concerted effort to drop these likes (to which we are attached) and dislikes that we want to avoid at any cost.

The Hindu scripture the Bhagavad Gita emphasizes this quality above all else for one to remain tranquil through life. When you are attached to something or some person strongly, it becomes a binding desire, and when it is not fulfilled, anger ensues. The Gita tells us that this anger can become all-consuming when it stays for too long and takes over your rational thinking. Once you lose this critical aspect of human life, you are doomed to live a stressful existence and even lose your sanity. Similarly, a strong dislike can make you start to hate the person who caused (or seems to have caused) a situation to happen, and again, your life is full of stress and you lose control of yourself. We can trace all hate crimes to this quality in a human being, and it not only affects the individual but the society in which this person lives. The rise of hate crimes against people of different backgrounds, religions, and ethnicities is at an all-time high in the United States and tarnishes the reputation of the whole country and the communities in which it happens.

The best way I know to remain stress-free can be summarized as follows:

- Manage your likes and dislikes, and make them into preferences.
- Analyze your guilt and hurt by introspection, and take action to address them directly instead of letting them fester in your mind.
- Accept what happens in your life by reducing your expectations of others. Accept the results of your works and actions, be they good, bad, or indifferent, since you deserve what you get. This is the universal law of God.
- Spend some quiet time every day with yourself so that you can look inward and learn form your experiences. This could take the form of meditation, reading scriptures, or just time without you being absorbed in the electronic devices that surround you.
- Follow a regular schedule and do everything in moderation—eating, sleeping, talking, working, exercising, etc. By doing this, you remain healthy, cheerful, and tranquil.
- Be compassionate and help others in need. In this way, your own worries seem trivial and you receive joy from the happiness you see in those you help. Many people compare themselves with others who they feel are doing better than they are, rather than being aware of how much they have that others in society lack. Remember you are unique and should not compare yourself with anyone else.

By following these simple steps, I've remained stress-free throughout my career and in my retirement. I maintain good health and am able to enjoy life fully. In my retirement, I keep myself busy helping others and spend time in nature with daily walks. I also devote time to reading the scriptures and meditating daily. I feel sure you can do the same—or something similar, in your own way!

Start Now by Integrating the 9 Steps into Your Life

This book started by describing nine values that can form the basis of your life. Prioritizing these values and finding no excuses to deviate from them will help you begin a stress-free life. Living a life founded on values prepares you mentally and emotionally to undertake the 9 Steps detailed in essay 2. This is called Dharmic living in Hinduism, and some variety of ethical living in the scriptures of most all other traditions.

Here's how you can integrate the 9 Steps into your daily life.

Discipline is the mark of any successful man or woman in the world. With discipline, you will do what has to be done and not put off things, allowing yourself to be stress-free. There is a saying in Hindi, the national language of India: "Do what you have to do today by not procrastinating until later in the day. Plan well for tomorrow." By doing this, you have no guilt from procrastination and last-minute stress-filled moments to reach a deadline. Discipline has been the centerpiece of my life, and my day is tranquil. You can achieve success in your career, and relations with others are maintained. You can take time on the weekends to catch up with friends and other family members and get ready for the next week. Discipline is needed to achieve anything in life, and each person can use their own methods to develop discipline and run a meaningful life, instead of being dictated to by the stresses of the moment. Managing your mind and not letting the mind manage you is the key ingredient of discipline.

Being true to yourself is a trait that can keep you free of guilt and regrets. In *On the Brink of Everything*, Parker Palmer quotes from Catholic writer and activist Thomas Merton and says that one has to make a distinction between true self and false self.[33] The true self is the source of that inner voice that keeps saying what is the right thing for you, and you have to listen to it carefully to lead an ethical stress-free life. In another Merton quote, he says that most of us "live lives of self-impersonation." If we do this, we fool ourselves, although we might feel we are fooling others. In the long run, it just builds stress and ruins your happiness. Alert living, where we monitor our thoughts, words, and actions deliberately, will help you be true to yourself.

I have done business in the United States and India, and when I meet with people the first time, I tell them, "Say what you mean and mean what you say," then we will have an honest and thriving business relationship. I had to buy out a joint venture partnership I had in India when I found out that the owner of the other company was telling me something that I didn't see in action on the ground when I visited the India office. The staff in the India office complained to me that my partner wasn't paying their salaries or travel reimbursements on time. This was causing stress in their lives, and they were not able to be fully productive in the office. When I asked the partner about this, he just covered it up and made some excuses that didn't make sense. So I took steps to buy out his portion of the company, and since then, the India office has been doing well and growing by leaps and bounds.

Putting health first is something some of us know and some of us have to learn. "Health is wealth" is a saying I have heard since I was a young boy. I was always conscious of my health and I could do the things I wanted to do. However, when I started my business in my late thirties, I

---

33 Parker Palmer, *On the Brink of Everything: Grace, Gravity, and Getting Old* (Berrett-Koehler Publishers, 2018).

started working very hard to build my business and also started going to law school in the evenings. I began neglecting exercise and proper eating habits, and my health deteriorated. I had to be rushed to an emergency room, and after two weeks, I got back to normal. That event revealed to me that whatever else I had to do, I could not neglect my health.

Since that time, I have put my health first and taken care to eat a proper diet and get regular exercise. I have maintained good health and feel like I'm in my sixties although I am in my seventies. I advise all young people that although you may think you are invincible in your twenties and thirties, a pattern of inconsistent eating and exercise will catch up with you in your forties and fifties. The body ages, and if you don't maintain it in good condition, it will give you problems. We spend time maintaining our cars and homes but neglect our health due to other pressures in life. So putting health first and maintaining good physical and mental health are essential to living a tranquil and purposeful life. We have all kinds of help from medical experts on how to eat right, exercise, and get enough sleep. We have apps to monitor our exercise and fitness. We have to use these and be cognizant of our health at all times. Regular health checkups with your doctor cannot be ignored if you want to live a stress-free life.

Our attitude toward work has more lifelong consequences than many of us initially realize. Work takes up 40 to 60 hours every week, and if we are not happy with the work we do, it affects our health and our productivity. At an early age, I was taught that if I treat work as a worship to the God who helped me get the education and qualifications for the work, it would be fun and I could put forward my best effort. As adults, it's helpful to look at work as our contribution to society and as payback for the amenities society provides us, such as good schools and colleges that train us. Many times, we expect things from our boss and our coworkers, and if these expectations are not met, we get frustrated and blame others instead of analyzing what we could do to improve the results of our work. We may postpone things that need to be done, and when deadlines approach, we panic and can't put forth our best effort.

I have been in several fields of work, from starting my career in mining (for which I went to college) and ending up as an environmental manager (which I learned along the way), cleaning up water and soil. In all aspects of my work, I saw myself as contributing to the economy and was excited to get up and start my work. This attitude of contributing to the community's welfare was a driver that kept me happy and productive throughout my 44-year career.

To the many young people I work with, I urge that their objective in finding the right job should not be on the financial compensation the job offers but on the challenges it offers and how it can make them a true contributor in their field of expertise. Money does not buy happiness; it is only a tool for acquiring some creature comforts. So if our attitude is to improve ourselves daily and build strong relationships at work that will help us do our work well, we'll enjoy going to work every day. The result of any work can be what you expect, worse than you expect, or better than you expect. So you can't let the result of your work dictate your attitude toward work. You can only do your best and know that the result depends on many factors over which you have little or no control. This attitude toward work allows you to be stress-free and to remain tranquil even after a busy day.

Daily meditation and quiet time were part of the focus of this book's essays on the scientific and the spiritual bases of tranquility, each essay describing how these mental practices contribute to a tranquil life. Scientific studies, for example, have proved definitively that daily meditation or taking quiet time aside for reflection have a significant effect on the brain chemistry and networks that help us manage our need for instant gratification and maintain our composure even during stressful situations. The longer the habit of daily meditation continues (even for 20 minutes a day), the greater the increase seen in benefits, as was evident in the brain wave patterns of long-term meditators such as Buddhist monks. Because of my own years of twice-daily breathing exercises and meditation, I've remained healthy despite chronic childhood asthma. And it's also allowed me to do my daily exercise and preserve my calm during several stressful situations in my career.

Just as the human body needs sleep to recover physically for the next day's activities, the human mind needs daily quiet time for it to function effectively. In the modern digital age of constant screen time with our cell phone, computer, iPad, and television sets, mental quiet time is all the more important. I emphasize to my daughter, a busy lawyer, who doesn't turn off her devices until she has to go to bed, that at least 15 minutes of quiet time is essential when she shuts off her devices. That will allow her a good night's sleep.

Our minds are overloaded with information from news podcasts, top stories that pop up on our cell phone, and emails (including *lots* of spam) and cell phone messages that greet us on waking up. We keep getting notifications of the above, and the urge to check them immediately has become second nature. I've developed a basic approach to managing my cell phone and computer use, and it consists of this:

1. Not checking any messages till I've had my morning shower and finished my prayers

2. Responding to email in the morning, and not checking my phone again until lunchtime
3. After lunch, responding to my messages and emails, and finishing the day by about 6:00 p.m.
4. Turning off my phone after dinner and not turning it on again until the next morning

This might not work for everyone, but you can develop your own way of managing information overload. The main idea is for us to control our digital devices instead of them calling the shots. My method hasn't alienated me from my friends and family since they all know my routine and respect it. I'm still able to attend meetings and do a lot of voluntary work during my retirement, and at the end of each day, I'm stress-free and tranquil. Daily meditation has been a great source of joy and happiness in my life, and I wish the same for you. It has kept me productive, as well as connected to my spiritual roots.

Work-life balance has become a popular catch phrase in the recent past, but many people are hard-pressed to say just what they mean by it. We've established elsewhere that work is an important part of life that can give us a sense of dignity and purpose. Say it occupies about one-third of our weekday, with the rest of that day (besides the time we sleep) left for us to fulfill our other roles in life.

Many workaholics neglect their time with family and friends, and they often come to regret it later in life when they can't do anything about it. At that point, family members and friends have usually moved on with their own lives, leaving the former workaholics to lead a lonely solitary old age. Arthur Brooks, in his book *From Strength to Strength*,[34] says that "[what] workaholics truly crave is not work per se but the success it brings. They kill themselves working for money, power, and prestige because they are forms of approval, applause, and compliments—which, like all addictive things, from cocaine to social media, stimulate the neurotransmitter dopamine." He cites many stories of people who have felt frustrated and empty after a career in which they have spent their life chasing success and finally come to realize that spending more time with family and spiritual pursuits is more fulfilling and gives them more of the happiness that they were after originally. In our competitive world of digital information overload, this kind of work-life balance is essential for health and serenity.

Early in my career, I learned that work-life balance is essential. My boss in my first job out of college made a point of this, telling me that people who stay long after work hours are just not efficient in getting their work done and that I should learn to manage my time and not spend more than forty to forty-five hours per week at work. I developed interests such as tennis and travel, as well as spending time with friends and family on weekends. Later in my career, I enjoyed volunteering, especially giving back to my community (both in the U.S. and in India, from where I immigrated in 1970). All this activity has served me well in retirement, too, as I keep busy with volunteering. The sense of joy I feel when I see someone succeed with whom I have shared my time and talents is immense. The work-life balance I developed helped me succeed in my career because I was never burnt out and approached every workday with enthusiasm and cheer.

---

34 Arthur C. Brooks, *From Strength to Strength: Finding Success, Happiness, and Deep Purpose in the Second Half of Life* (Portfolio, 2022).

To **serve others** operates as a central value in all of the world's major spiritual traditions. The Bhagavad Gita, the Hindu scripture that has been my lifelong guide, emphasizes that all of us are on this planet to help each other and that by finding opportunities to serve, you can have a purposeful life. My grandmother taught me that service to humanity is service to God, since God exists not in temples but in the infinite variety of humans, plants, and animals He has created.

My love of the environment and of conserving natural resources comes from this belief system. During college, I helped other students in understanding the subjects we were taught. At work, I always loved to mentor young engineers to be their best. On evenings and weekends, I found opportunities to tutor students from Chicago public schools who were falling behind in their class. I met other volunteers along the way who introduced me to the needs of society in the areas of hunger and environmental protection projects. Working with these volunteers, I enjoyed becoming fully involved with the Greater Chicago Food Depository, which serves some 800,000 needy Cook County citizens. I continued doing this during my career and retirement, and have never known a dull moment in my life.

Serving others is your moral and social responsibility as a citizen of any community—which may make it sound somber and onerous. But in fact, like me, you will doubtless find much joy in this service. The United States is full of service opportunities that are filled by community volunteers. And without their valuable efforts, many people would suffer, because the government social safety net is not enough. As a member of the Lions Club in my community, I can testify to the joy that the Lions logo "We Serve" reflects in all its 1.4 million volunteers worldwide. Similarly, Rotary and other service organizations around the U.S. excel in offering ready assistance to strangers during disasters, relief after disasters, and day-to-day caring for the poor and elderly in communities. International relief organizations around the world offer help to refugees and poor children and adults facing various difficulties in their lives. I belong to Engineers Without Borders in Chicago; and engineers and other volunteers in 35 countries help communities around the world gain access to clean water and sanitation, solar power, improved schools, and upgraded roads and bridges. Doctors Without Borders serve the sick and wounded worldwide. These acts of service make humanity better and the world a better place. So you can volunteer as well and, in turn, enjoy the tranquility and happiness it can help you achieve.

To **live a purposeful life** was the theme at the heart of Victor Frankl's work as described in essay 3. His efforts to find meaning in his life took place in more challenging circumstances than most of ours have or will experience, since he was at the time suffering in the Auschwitz concentration camp during World War II. However, his exhortation to all of us is still relevant, and it is that without purpose in our lives, we can easily lose hope and give up, even under the routine difficulties we face in life. So finding purpose and striving to achieve that purpose irrespective of the difficulties we face in life underlies all human pursuits. If that purpose encompasses the welfare of the whole society in which you are placed, the joy of life is further enhanced. Even if the purpose is to do your job well and be of help to others in your family, you will strive with hope every day and work hard.

Based on his long experience as a social scientist and professor at Harvard Business School, Arthur Brooks, again in *From Strength to Strength*, lists three priorities by which to live:

- Use things.
- Love people.
- Worship the Divine.

He says that "if you love things, you will strive to objectify yourself in terms of money, power, pleasure and prestige. You will worship yourself [and end up unhappy, although the world seems to place an inordinate level of importance on these]." For me, worshipping the Divine has always meant helping the poor who need help from society, as taught by my grandmother. The level of tranquility and happiness I have achieved is immeasurable, and I constantly find opportunities to serve in areas such as clean water, hunger alleviation, and education.

It can be tricky to **always see the big picture**. Many of us get bogged down in our daily lives of problems and never lift ourselves from these problems to look at the big picture. But once you decide to see the big picture—to step out of your narrow perspective within your own life and view yourself within the wider perspective of your family, your community, society, and beyond—you learn to count your blessings and not focus on smaller problems that keep you stuck in a cycle of happiness and sorrow. As we saw above, working to serve others and to live a purposeful life can channel us away from a preoccupation with our personal problems and turn our attention to other, more productive opportunities. Each of the steps in this book contributes to the cumulative effect of making us tranquil, and as we master each step, our self-confidence and tranquility increase significantly. When you don't see the big picture, you can hurt others while pursuing your selfish, narrow goals in life. History is replete with stories of people who pursued their selfish goals and, in the end, died unhappy and were soon forgotten. However, we know of ordinary people who were willing to help others and were celebrated as heroes by their community.

As with my own story of fretting about my grades in school and not enjoying my youth, it's easy to overfocus on your problem and lose sight of what lies ahead. Once I learned to put aside the narrower focus, I could achieve my goals and go on to a great career in engineering and service to others. So by stepping back from your problems and seeing the big picture that lies ahead of you, you can achieve the impossible (or what you thought was impossible). I remind my daughter every time she gets stressed at work or in her personal life that this too shall pass and brighter days are ahead. When she finishes tackling the immediate problem at hand and starts to smile, I remind her that her sole focus on her current problems made her forget all the wonderful things going on in her life. She has now understood how to change her focus to the big picture and is leading a successful life as a lawyer and a person who is able to use her legal skills to help others in need.

I Wish You Success in Achieving Tranquility

It is my sincere hope that the stories I've related from my life and history will help you follow this book's 9 Steps and achieve tranquility in all your pursuits. A calm mind, undisturbed by changing situations, is capable of achieving anything it wants, and this is why it is important to put in the hard and disciplined work it takes to achieve a tranquil mind and be in control of your life, instead of having a turbulent mind that can destroy you. And here is a final tip that has served me throughout my life: Persistence and patience will help you achieve what you want, so never give up and keep working toward your goal of a tranquil life.

ACKNOWLEDGMENTS

I WOULD LIKE TO THANK my wife, Usha Rajaram, for being there for me throughout my efforts to complete this book. She has spared countless valuable hours on my behalf over the last three years.

I would also like to thank my brother, Sri Vasudevan, for giving me so many good suggestions and sending me books that were indispensable references to my writing.

My ongoing thanks to my teachers, including my spiritual teachers, who have imparted to me important values and provided guidance during my journey to become a tranquil person. They have instilled in me the strong self-discipline that has become second nature over the many years of my life.

And my enduring gratitude to my parents and my paternal grandparents, who infused in me the notion that service to humanity is service to God. They were my guiding lights throughout my early childhood and youth.

I wish to offer a two-part thanks, first to Judith West for her excellent editorial help and for making sure that I accurately relayed all the quotations I have used in this book. I want to thank her, too, for referring me to editor Kim Bookless, whose teammates at The Cadence Group and GKS Creative guided me through the design and printing phases of this book.

In addition, my thanks to my friend Elizabeth Jumah and my cousin Chandra Prabha, who read the initial manuscripts and provided feedback to improve the book.

Last but certainly not least, my deep appreciation to my daughter, Pooja Rajaram, who inspired me to write this book and has helped me develop tranquility skills, especially during her teenage years. She became a friend to me as she reached adulthood and has been a sounding partner to me as I wrote this book.

ABOUT THE AUTHOR

DR. RAJARAM is a retired engineer who has practiced Tranquility for the last 35 years and has written this book to help professionals who are experiencing stress from work or other issues in their lives. He has lived both in India (till age 22) and the United States. He provides practical advice on how to stay calm and remain happy in this fast-paced digital age.

He obtained graduate degrees in engineering (masters and doctorate) from the South Dakota School of Mines and Technology and University of Wisconsin, respectively. He got his undergraduate from Osmaia University in India. He also has a Juris Doctor from the Kent College of Law in Chicago. He has run successful businesses in Chicago and New Delhi, India.

Since retirement, he has been active in various nonprofit organizations. These include the Lions Club of Burr Ridge-Hinsdale-Oak Brook, Engineers Without Borders in Chicago, and Sonoma Ashram in California. He is now working on Sustainable Development projects in Bungoma, western Kenya.

He is the author of six books, including *Golden Giving* (Amazon, 2017) and *Climate Change and Environment* (Notion Press, 2022).

www.ingramcontent.com/pod-product-compliance
Lightning Source LLC
Chambersburg PA
CBHW070858160726
48004CB00003B/1142